BONE VOYAGE
Travel with Your Pet

Mary-Alice Pomputius

dog jaunt BOOKS

BONE VOYAGE: TRAVEL WITH YOUR PET

A Dog Jaunt® Book
Published in the United States by Fair Prospect Press

December 2013 edition

Cover design and illustrations: Chandler O'Leary
Interior design: Walter Smith
Set in Arno, Myriad, and Trajan

ISBN 978-1-941078-00-6

About this book

My name is Mary-Alice Pomputius, and I
write a dog travel blog called Dog Jaunt.
Since 2009, I've been recording every
scrap of information I've learned as I've
traveled with Chloe, our Cavalier King
Charles Spaniel. I encourage you to read
and follow Dog Jaunt, and join in the
community that's grown up around it
by sharing your own dog travel experiences. But what you want right now is
a book — organized and thorough, but
relatively brief — about traveling with a
pet. *Bone Voyage* gathers together the best
and most useful dog travel information
and tips, letting you know about the
most enjoyable pet-friendly destinations,
how to prepare for your trip together,
and how to keep your pet safe and
happy while you're away from home.

   Bone Voyage has been over a year in
the making. I originally wrote it for
Frommer's, the venerable travel guide
company. As the publishing date neared,
Frommer's was purchased by Google,
and their e-book projects were cancelled.
While I was initially devastated — what
timing! — I'm now grateful for how
things turned out. I would have loved the
association with the Frommer's brand
(the first time I traveled to Europe, my
parents were still using their dog-eared
Europe on $5 a Day, and my family stuck
by Arthur as the dollar figure slid upwards
over the years to $25), but self-publishing
means that I can issue revisions whenever
I feel it's necessary, and lets me speak
in my own voice, including giving you
some rule-bending suggestions the
Frommer's editor was hesitant to include.

Praise for Bone Voyage

"With this book, you'll learn about the most pet-friendly destinations — the best cities, airlines, hotels, and restaurants. You'll know what to pack, how to keep your pet safe and happy, and all the proper travel 'petiquette.' Whether you're flying to Europe or just taking a car trip, you'll want this book."

— Gene Openshaw
co-author of Rick Steves guidebooks and walking tour e-books

I discovered this author through her blog, Dog Jaunt, then through Facebook. They were life-savers when I wanted to take our first puppy on his first trip! This book has all the same info plus tons more, and contains links to new info on related websites so that you'll always have access to the latest data. I could not recommend this more highly.

— Kate W.

I've long been a fan of DogJaunt.com, Mary-Alice Pomputius' pet travel website. Bone Voyage expands upon the information found on the website and presents it in a well organized package. There are helpful links to important documents, resources and publications. Bone Voyage is an essential read If you've ever contemplated traveling with your pet.

— Jenna E.

Praise for Dog Jaunt

"I just wanted to give you a HUGE THANK YOU for your website and how informative/detailed it is. I have a Maltese/Bichon mix and it tears my heart to leave my 10 y/o child behind when I travel and finding sitters is extremely difficult as she cannot be boarded or around other dogs due to health issues. With all the information on your site, I was given new hope. I am confident we will travel with zero issues. I feel like we've already done lots of traveling by reading your blogs as it makes me feel like I know exactly what to expect at all stages of travel. You're a Godsend!"

— Briana M. and Hailey-bug

"I have found a wealth of helpful information on your blog. It has soothed my nerves and helped me find answers to many, many questions that I have had about traveling with my little Abby. We have a number of trips planned for this year. I am grateful for all the info and advice about airline carriers. I was also thrilled to find the information on public transit systems. Thank you!"

— Carol L.

"I came across Dog Jaunt about 3 years ago when I was searching the web for the best dog carriers to travel with my then 1-year-old dog Jazz-Min to Canada and France. I found that your blog was by far the most useful source of information in this regard and I learned so much from you about the best ways to travel internationally. Jazz-Min is now a seasoned traveler, having been to France and Canada 2 times already in the last 3 years! Thank you for all your help in every aspect of air-traveling with a dog!"

— Anne B.

"I can't tell you how happy I was when I discovered your blog! I had been traveling with my little Papillon, Molly, for a few years when I came across Dog Jaunt. I spent the next few hours reading and reading. I really appreciate the recommendations for dog friendly accommodations and restaurants. I also love that readers can contribute their own experiences with travel."

— Jen V.

"This is the ONLY blog I read on a regular basis, and am always looking forward to the next post. You have done a great job creating an on-line community, making me feel that Alfie and I are not alone in battling airlines, airports, and the ever-stressful TSA...."

— Gery O.

"Thank you for all the work you have put into compiling all this information! Thank you for being a life saver when traveling, a calmer of airport storms, a saver of my sanity in all things doggy travel and airline rules and regulations! Not to mention all the wonderful dog friendly restaurants, sights and places to stay you have compiled for everyone to share. Don't know what I'd do without you!! <3 you guys!"

— Heike G.

"We adopted a small dog specifically so we could travel in-cabin with him, but we knew nothing about how to actually do that. Thankfully, we discovered this blog. We've now flown successfully with Wrigley on a number of occasions, and our trips have been made much, much easier because of information learned from you and the community you have created."

— Amanda D.

He is a good friend and traveling companion, and would rather travel about than anything he can imagine. If he occurs at length in this account, it is because he contributed much to the trip. A dog, particularly an exotic like Charley, is a bond between strangers.

John Steinbeck,
Travels with Charley: In Search of America

Contents

Introduction 1
Keeping Bone Voyage Fur-esh 3

CHAPTER 1 **Paws and reflect: An overview of pet travel 5**
Where can a traveler with a pet go? 5
Will traveling with a pet limit me? 5
How hard is it to travel with a pet? 6
Tips for traveling with pets other than dogs 6

CHAPTER 2 **The best dog-friendly destinations 9**
City-based vacations 10
Leave the city behind 11

CHAPTER 3 **Digs: Finding a dog-friendly hotel 15**
Hotel chains and groups 15
History buffs and luxury lovers 16
Useful travel websites 16
Vacation rentals 17
Hotel and house guest etiquette and safety 18

CHAPTER 4 **Bone appetit: Finding dog-friendly restaurants 21**
Finding a dog-friendly U.S. restaurant 21
Eating with your dog in Europe 22
Eating with your dog down under 22
Restaurant petiquette 23

CHAPTER 5 **Ruff road: Driving with your pet 25**
Keeping your pet safe in the car 25
Making a car trip comfortable 27
Pet-friendly car rentals and shares 28
Traveling in an RV with a pet 28

CHAPTER 6 **Bus, train, and boat 31**
Bark of the bus: Traveling by coach with your pet 31
Making tracks: Traveling by train with your pet 32
Poop deck: Sailing with your pet 35

CHAPTER 7 **Tail wind: Flying with your pet 41**
Before you travel 41
On the day of travel 46

CHAPTER 8 **On foot and by bike 51**
Walking and hiking with your pet 51
Pet-togethers: Dog parks and meet-ups 53
Biking with your dog 54

CHAPTER 9 **Three pees: Preparation, Paperwork and Packing 55**
Preparing your pet for travel 55
Paperwork 56
Selecting and packing the best pet travel gear 63

CHAPTER 10 **Troubleshooting 69**
Motion sickness and anxiety 69
Pets with special needs 70
Breed ban pets 70
Feeding your pet away from home 71
Clothing for demanding weather 72
Preparing for medical emergencies 72
Ensuring that your lost pet is returned to you 74
No faux paws: Being a responsible pet owner 75

APPENDIX A **Airline Policies 77**
U.S. In-Cabin Pet Travel 78
International In-Cabin Pet Travel 81
U.S. Checked/Cargo Pet Travel 86
International Checked/Cargo Pet Travel 88

APPENDIX B **Recommended reading 95**
Pet travel guides 95
Pet-friendly vacation ideas 95
First Aid guides 95
Scraps 96

Introduction

We were standing on a crowded bus in Paris, staggering and swaying as we headed back to our rented apartment in the Marais. Chloe, our young Cavalier King Charles Spaniel, was tucked into my new dog tote (a handsome gray felt number that I still haven't seen in the U.S.). Near us, sitting in the seats reserved for people who really deserve to be sitting down, was a lady well past a certain age, burdened with a purse and a shopping basket. A few blocks into our trip, she caught my eye and urgently offered to swap places with me. I refused, of course, but the exchange — nearly mute, but full of smiles and politeness and good cheer — made my day. Such kindness, in a city that's been bearing with clueless tourists for millenia! I owed it entirely to Chloe, peeking over the edge of her fabulous tote, and indeed, she made that entire trip a delight.

Why travel with a pet? For many people, their animal companion is a vital part of their ability to handle health issues and participate fully in their communities. They travel with their service animal because they do everything with him. A growing number of people, however, are *choosing* to travel with their *pet* — and for the same reasons that prompted them to get a pet in the first place. They find their pet comforting and amusing. They like how caring for him requires them to get on their feet and out the door. Why leave all that companionship behind when you go on vacation?

The basic reason for traveling with your pet is that it makes you happy to be with him and he loves being with you. Another good reason? You may well save money, given the cost of boarding your pet in a kennel, or hiring a pet sitter. And here's a reason you'll have to take on faith, until you've made your first trip together: A vacation with your pet is more fun than one without.

Cities are best absorbed at a walking pace, and with a dog you'll be walking at least a couple of times a day. Worried about culture shock or isolation? It's difficult to be depressed, and impossible to be lonely, when your pet is with you. Pets are natural ambassadors, too: No city will seem unfriendly when you've just shared a laugh with another dog owner whose leash has been braided with yours by your dogs' antics. (Other kinds of traveling are an even easier sell, since hiking and camping are much more fun with a pet, as are road trips.)

The argument you will hear most often *against* pet travel is that it's unfair to your pet, and that he'd rather remain behind than undergo the stress of travel. I believe, however, that anyone who is paying close attention to their pet will have a good sense of how he's reacting to a situation, and whether he is comfortable and happy — or not. The signals a pet sends through his posture, his body language, the way he holds his ears and tail, and the expression in his eyes are easily interpreted by an attentive owner. You are one of those owners, or you wouldn't have purchased this book. You may already know how your pet feels about travel, if you've taken some short trips with him. You can decide for yourself — and him — what he prefers. It is by no means self-indulgent to travel with a pet. For both you and your pet, it may be a wonderful choice.

This book contains hundreds of links to helpful resources on the Web. Unfortunately, you can't just tap your finger on the page to follow a link in a printed book, but I've tried to make it almost that easy: Just type the short code following the link into your Web browser's address bar. For example, to follow this link to my blog Dog Jaunt jnt.im/106, you'd enter "jnt.im/106" in your web browser.

A large part of the reason that I provide so many links is that I don't want to get you (or me) into trouble. Things change, even more rapidly than I can issue new revisions of this book, so I strongly encourage you to verify for yourself that the information I've provided is still accurate. There's no money to be made from blogging, or even selling a book, so I won't be able to reimburse you for tickets you find you suddenly can't use!

Throughout the book, you'll find links to specific providers (including hotels) and products (including carriers, crates, water bottles, and other gear). I have not been paid to recommend any products or include these links. The gear I provide links for is all gear that I use and like (or admire, in the case of gear for birds and other exotic pets). Because I like to keep things transparent, you should know that I do get a small kick-back if you buy gear through the Amazon links I provide.

KEEPING BONE VOYAGE FUR-ESH

The most important thing I've learned from writing the Dog Jaunt blog is that I learn as much from my readers as they do from me. Please help me keep *Bone Voyage* current and useful by sending me comments, corrections, and updates via email at books@dogjaunt.com

This is the December 2013 edition of *Bone Voyage*. To see if there is a newer version, and to register for email notifications of updates to the book, please visit the Books section of dogjaunt.com.

I plan to update the book frequently, but between editions, you can find updates to the information in the book at www.dogjaunt.com/updates.

1

Paws and reflect: An overview of pet travel

Let's start with the most basic question: What kind of pets can travel? Most traveling pets are dogs, and the ones who fly frequently are typically small dogs. It's less common to encounter a traveler with another kind of pet, but they certainly exist (particularly including cats, but also birds, ferrets, hamsters, guinea pigs, and rabbits). This guide focuses on traveling dogs, but owners of other pets should also find it helpful.

WHERE CAN A TRAVELER WITH A PET GO?

Where there's a will, there's a way, as the saying goes. People have traveled around parts of Africa jnt.im/576 in a Land Rover with their dog, and they've taken their dog to Machu Picchu jnt.im/577. Pets are not allowed at all in Antarctica, but that leaves you six continents to explore. That said, you'd likely want to avoid countries where dogs and cats are regarded as ingredients (primarily China, Korea, and Vietnam), and countries where contact with dogs is a religious taboo jnt.im/575. Some countries (e.g., Australia, New Zealand) have stringent quarantine requirements, which may not work with your schedule.

This guide focuses on travel in, and between, North America and Western Europe. For cultural and economic reasons, those regions have the most pet-friendly airlines, trains, public transit systems, hotels, restaurants, activities and caregivers — and are therefore where pet travel is easiest. You will be given the tools you need, however, to take the road less traveled.

WILL TRAVELING WITH A PET LIMIT ME?

Since you love your pet, I suspect you're prepared to believe that it would be fun to vacation with her. But will having her along prevent you from experiencing everything your destination has to offer? What about the museums? The cathedrals? The theaters?

Some cathedrals will turn a blind eye to a small pet in an over-the-shoulder carrier, but your question is a good one: Does it make sense to take a pet to a place

Recognizing their unique skills and training, lawmakers around the world have smoothed the way for service animals to stay by their owners' sides. They are allowed everywhere (or nearly everywhere) their owners choose to go. This guide focuses not on service animals but on pets, who have more restrictions to deal with.

Because the service animal certification process is insufficiently regulated, it is possible to game the system by putting a fake service vest on your pet (and, for flyers, coaxing a supporting letter out of a doctor). I am strongly opposed to this maneuver, since it does a terrible disservice to real working dogs and their owner companions. Their position in our culture is still fragile enough to be harmed by the hijinks of a comparatively untrained pet. I bend some rules (and I will alert you when I'm doing it), but I do not recommend this gimmick.

where she won't be able to be with you every moment? The answer is yes. You, after all, will only be spending a fraction of your vacation in museums and theaters. Plan ahead, and take your dog for a long walk in the morning — and then go to the museum while she's napping. Or take a long walk in the afternoon, and let her snooze while you go to the theater.

HOW HARD IS IT TO TRAVEL WITH A PET?

It depends on where you want to go (and where you're starting from), and what kind of pet you're traveling with. Taking a dog by car from the U.S. to Canada, or by ferry from the U.K. to Ireland, is a walk in the park. Taking a bird from South Africa to Australia isn't allowed; if your pet is a dog, she'll be in quarantine for the better part of a year. Those are the extremes; in between, you'll find yourself facing varying quantities of on-line research, paperwork, and preparation/packing. *Bone Voyage* will let you know where to do the research, and how to get the paperwork completed. You'll learn what you need to do to prepare your pet for travel, and what gear and products will improve your pet's travel experience.

In many of the world's most popular destinations, business owners are responding to an increased interest in pet travel by offering a slew of pet-friendly amenities. It is now very easy to find a pet-friendly hotel, and it's increasingly easy to find pet-friendly restaurants (especially when the weather is mild and you can eat at an outdoor patio).

Pets are more often than not allowed on public transit (small pets in carriers have an easier time of it than big dogs), small pets in carriers that fit under the seat can travel in-cabin on many airlines (dogs and cats have an easier time of it than more exotic pets), and pets can travel on most European trains.

More shops than you'd guess allow leashed pets inside. Pet care providers are increasingly easy to find, to help you with your pet's medical needs away from home, or to entertain your pet for an afternoon if you're doing something she can't be a part of. People continue to spend handsomely on their pets, so it's generally easy to find a pet store within a reasonable distance — meaning that you don't have to carry with you every scrap of food your pet will eat on a trip.

With a little planning and research (and this book, of course), traveling with your pet is a straightforward proposition — and so enjoyable that you, like us, will look forward to seeing your next destination at the end of a leash.

TIPS FOR TRAVELING WITH PETS OTHER THAN DOGS

Only one of our family's **cats** travels, and we keep his trips brief. There are cats who relish travel jnt.im/117, and if yours is one of them, you'll be able to bring her in-cabin with you on most airlines. Since she's small enough to fit in a pet carrier, she'll also be allowed on most public transit systems. Your main concerns are likely to be handling her litter box needs and finding accommodations that welcome cats as well as dogs.

Birds can readily be taught to tolerate a leash and harness (to prevent a sudden, startled departure from your shoulder), and bird diapers jnt.im/116 will prevent messes, giving you more flexibility in your schedule. Bird backpacks (waist packs are available for small birds) give your pet shelter on your back or shoulder, at your waist, or strapped into a car. Many birds will fit comfortably into an in-cabin carrier, and most airlines will let your bird travel in-cabin with you — but you will need to look a little harder to find hotels that welcome birds, and you will have to grapple with special rules regulating the import/export of pet birds. This article jnt.im/118 has good, basic information about traveling with a bird.

Ferrets can be delicate pets: They are prone to a number of diseases, and they don't tolerate heat well. You will want to choose destinations with easy access to good medical care. They may nip, especially when startled, so be cautious about letting your pet be handled by strangers, and carry copies of her rabies vaccination record with you. They're clever and nimble creatures — keep a wary eye on your pet in a soft carrier to see if she digs, or can outsmart the zippers, and if so, choose a small hard-sided carrier like the PetMate Cabin Kennel jnt.im/113, with a wire top so you can keep an eye on your girl. Ferrets are banned as pets in a couple of U.S. states and in several other jurisdictions; you'll want to avoid vacationing in those areas. Again, you'll need to search a little harder for hotels that will welcome your pet. Currently, no airlines will allow a ferret to travel in-cabin with you. For advice about traveling with a ferret, I recommend starting with this article jnt.im/112 from Ferret News, and this guide jnt.im/114 from Massachusetts Ferret Friends.

Traveling with **rodents** like hamsters and guinea pigs is fairly straightforward — their small size makes them easily portable, and the same food, water, exercise and bedding solutions that work at home can be packed to work on the road as well. Your main concerns will be finding hotels that accept a hamster or guinea pig, and finding airlines that will let your pet travel with you in-cabin (Frontier is the only U.S. option; Iberia may also allow hamsters and guinea pigs in cabin). Take a look at this blog post jnt.im/111 for advice about traveling with a hamster.

In the U.S., **rabbits** may travel in-cabin on Alaska, Continental/United, and Frontier; of the airlines based in other countries, Iberia might possibly allow rabbits in-cabin. Because they fit in a small carrier (the same PetMate Cabin Kennel jnt.im/115 that works for ferrets is also a good choice for most rabbits), they can travel with you on most public transit systems. A metal wire carrier designed specifically for rabbits jnt.im/109 will work better on road trips. Rabbits, like ferrets, can be trained to walk with a harness and leash jnt.im/110, which will let you take them out at rest areas on road trips. Litter box train jnt.im/107 your rabbit and you can use the same traveling litter box solutions that work for traveling cats and ferrets. Read this guide jnt.im/108 from the House Rabbit Society for advice about traveling with a rabbit.

2

The best dog-friendly destinations

The best destinations for travelers with dogs are those with opportunities for long, interesting walks (whether it's in the wild or in a fascinating streetscape), and with genuinely pet-friendly places to stay and eat. Pet-friendly public transit is a tremendous plus, as is a good supply of quality pet stores and pet care providers. It is a great delight when you're put to welcome to join you in stores as you window-shop, and in some destinations that's perfectly acceptable.

A tempting destination is also one that is easy to reach. "Easy" is a relative term, of course — but we can all agree that it is not easy to bring a pet to a country with stringent import requirements. If you live in Australia, you may well regard Sydney as a delightful pet-friendly destination, but visitors will find the Australian (and New Zealand) quarantine regulations daunting. Similarly, residents of the U.K. may gloat over the wealth of pet-friendly pubs and vacation lodging options available to them, but visitors arriving by air will need to decide whether they want to ship their pet as cargo, or if they will land with their in-cabin pet on the Continent (*e.g.,* in Paris or Amsterdam), and then make their way to the U.K. by ferry or car. Hawaii, too, poses hurdles to visitors with pets,

but it is possible, with advance footwork, to reduce your pet's quarantine time in Hawaii jnt.im/223 to just a few hours.

Destinations with a reputation for welcoming visitors with pets, especially dogs, include Paris (and France generally), Rome (and Italy), Berlin (and Germany), Vienna (and Austria), and Amsterdam (and the Netherlands). You and your dog may have to search a bit to find places to eat together in U.S. cities like New York, San Francisco, Seattle, Boston, Chicago, San Diego, and New Orleans, but you will readily find pet-friendly hotels, activities and public transit, especially if your pet is small. Similarly, London (and the U.K.), Stockholm (and Sweden), Copenhagen (and Denmark), Vancouver or Quebec (and Canada), and Buenos Aires are wonderful destinations if you are prepared to tuck your pet into a crate at your hotel during mealtime, if necessary. What you will find in all these places is a basic understanding that it is a desirable and pleasant thing to travel with a pet, and a shared appreciation of pets that will enhance your enjoyment of your trip.

The following is by no means an exhaustive list of the kinds of things you can do with your dog on vacation. It's meant to prime the pump — and to show you how unlimited your travel options are. Right now, I'm making plans for two very different kinds of trips with Chloe — one is city-based (a long stay in Paris) and the other is more rural (a walk along the length of Hadrian's Wall, the northern border of Roman Britain). Other kinds of trips you might consider are stays at a pet-friendly lodge or resort, or getaways where you and your dog can work together on a new skill.

CITY-BASED VACATIONS

It's easy to find a pet-friendly hotel (or, for longer stays, an apartment rental) in any of the cities I've listed, and they're all a delight to explore on foot and paw. For travelers with limited time, an urban vacation will be the best choice, since your plane will take you directly to your destination (except London, which will require a detour if you're traveling with an in-cabin pet).

EXAMPLE: PARIS

A trip to Paris will certainly include walking the city's streets (parks can be tricky — check this list jnt.im/224 to find out where your dog is welcome). You'll be able to buy groceries and prepared foods at the neighborhood open-air markets — dogs are not officially allowed, but seem to be universally tolerated. Your dog will be welcome in most shops (though not in grocery stores). He will also be able to join you in nearly every restaurant — and this will make all the difference to how you structure your day. No need to return to your apartment or hotel room before finding lunch! Instead, choose a place to eat after you've exercised your dog for a while, and he's ready to have a lie-down, and then continue wandering, after he's had a rest at your feet.

Are your dogs barking? Take a break from walking and see the city from the river: The Batobus jnt.im/220 allows leashed dogs (and pets in carriers) on board, and makes a relaxing loop around central Paris. Alternatively, tuck your pup into his tote bag and get on a bus (a regular bus jnt.im/221, I mean, not the pricey hop-on hop-off tourist buses). Route 69 is universally acknowledged to be scenic, but there are passionate supporters, too, of Routes 24, 29, 63, 72, 73, 87, and 95.

EXAMPLE: NEW YORK CITY

What better way to see the neighborhoods of Manhattan than by walking? Like Parisians, New Yorkers have a reputation for being brisk with tourists, but a visitor with a dog will see plenty of smiles (and a lot of other dogs and their people).

You and your dog will both love Central Park jnt.im/219, parts of which are even available for off-leash romping after 9 pm and before 9 am. Pack a book of walking tours, or find one on line (they're available for all interests). Bring a GPS device and a supply of small trinkets, and go geocaching jnt.im/222 — you'll enjoy the hunt, and your dog will enjoy the exercise. If your pet is portable, remember to bring a tote for him so you can take the subway or a bus when you want a break (buses wade slowly through traffic, but if you're weary, slow won't bother you; the M5 is fairly scenic, and I've enjoyed ambling down 5th Avenue on the M1, M2, M3, or M4 — especially during the holidays).

PARIS PETIQUETTE

Residents are reporting that it's not as commonplace as it was for your dog to enter a store or restaurant, so don't assume your pet is welcome. Pause by the door as you enter, and after you greet the proprietor and other shoppers/diners (a quiet but audible *"Bonjour, messieurs-dames"* will cover the whole establishment), ask if your pet can come in (*"Je peux entrer avec mon chien?"*). Say thank you and good-bye as you depart. This may sound overly-complicated, but Parisians will appreciate your good manners, and it may tip the balance in favor of your pet joining you.

Walk across the Brooklyn Bridge together (choose a mild day, wear comfortable shoes, and bring water for both of you — the round trip is about 2.5 miles). For stunning views without the effort, take the ferry to Staten Island and back jnt.im/218.

Have a world-class burger, fries and a shake at the Shake Shack in Madison Square Park jnt.im/225, or walk up to one of the city's food trucks (for current news and locations, follow @nycfoodtruck on Twitter). Step into Saks Fifth Avenue, or Tiffany, and buy something fabulous.

But the museums, you say! And the music, and the theater! How can I visit Paris without going to the Louvre? How can I miss the Met? There's no need to. Give your pet a good walk in the morning, and he'll doze happily in your room or apartment while you go places he can't. You can also find a dog walker or a day care center, even in cities much smaller than Paris and New York.

LEAVE THE CITY BEHIND

If you've had it up to *here* with city life, consider finding a pet-friendly vacation rental in a village in Tuscany or Provence or Cornwall, or on Ireland's Dingle Peninsula, and have your choice of cooking for yourself or finding a local restaurant or pub that will let your dog curl up at your feet. If you and your pup are looking for even more activity, find yourselves a working farm, or a dude ranch, or a getaway with access to cross-country skiing trails:

☞ Stay in a yurt at England's West Moss-side Farm jnt.im/215, an organic farm located by a nature preserve and offering yoga and art classes. On this side of the pond, the Huckleberry Tent and Breakfast jnt.im/214, 45 minutes east of Sandpoint, ID, offers three canvas tent cabins with queen beds, kitchen and wood stoves (plus outhouse and outdoor shower) — and a wealth of outdoor activities and beauty.

☞ Participate in the daily activities of an alpaca farm, or go hiking, biking and bird watching instead — the Champlain Valley Alpacas and Farmstay jnt.im/216 in Bridport, VT welcomes "well behaved dogs."

☞ Bring your dog with you to a dude ranch (or "guest ranch"). The Flying U Guest Ranch jnt.im/213 in British Columbia allows pet dogs in guest cabins and alongside you as you enjoy unsupervised riding on the ranch's many trails (make sure that your dog will stick by you, since other parties' horses, and the ranch's cattle, mustn't be spooked, and since there are frequent coyote spottings). Colorado's Sundance Trail Guest Ranch jnt.im/212 also welcomes pet dogs who can abide by the ranch's sensible list of rules. The Dude Ranchers' Association jnt.im/217 lists eighteen other pet-friendly U.S. dude ranches: To get the list, click on "Find a Ranch" by Amenities, then scroll down to "Ranch Policies" and click on "Pet Friendly".

☞ The Rolling Huts jnt.im/210 in eastern Washington's Methow Valley are cleverly designed, and put you and your pet in a perfect location for hiking and cross-country skiing.

☞ Go cross-country skiing with your buddy at Whistler Olympic Park jnt.im/211, a few miles away from Whistler Village, or stay at the Sleeping Lady jnt.im/209 resort in Leavenworth, WA, and cross-country ski or snowshoe from your cabin's door.

☞ Try skijoring (or canoeing, or hiking) together, with Toronto-based Dog Paddling Adventures jnt.im/226.

☞ Call Kayak Excursions jnt.im/204 (based in Maine, but offering rentals and tours in New York and Florida too) to arrange a dog-friendly kayak trip. Island Spirit Kayak jnt.im/205, on Martha's Vineyard, allows dogs in its rental kayaks (and will provide a doggy lifejacket too, if you tell them ahead of time your pup will be with you). On the other coast, Seattle's NWOC jnt.im/203 offers dog-friendly kayak rentals — grab your pup and explore Lake Union, Portage Bay, and the Arboretum.

☞ You and your dog can both run off-leash on the beautiful beach at Carmel-by-the-Sea (spend the night at Doris Day's Cypress Inn jnt.im/206, where you'll feel a little out of place if you *don't* have a pet).

☞ In Europe, Ryder-Walker Alpine Adventures jnt.im/201 will customize their self-guided tours (inns and luggage transport arranged for you) for hikers with dogs.

☞ Not feeling quite so athletic? Take a spa break with your pet at L'Auberge de Sedona jnt.im/202 or at the Lake Austin Spa Resort jnt.im/200.

☞ Go wine tasting with your furry foodie in Napa Valley jnt.im/207 and Sonoma jnt.im/198, Mendocino County jnt.im/199, the Pacific Northwest jnt.im/197, and New York's Finger Lakes jnt.im/208 region.

☞ Watch a ball game with your buddy, and let someone else do the running around: A search for "bark in the park"

will let you know when your favorite major or minor league baseball team is hosting a dog-friendly game.

PET-FRIENDLY RESORTS

The classic summer vacation for many of us was a couple of weeks spent at a lakeside lodge (or maybe it was called a "resort," but the places were shorts-and-bare-feet comfortable, not fancy). You spent all day outside doing stuff, coming back only for meals; you slept like a log; and the next day you did it again. Especially in the U.S., there are destinations that still offer vacations like that, and many of them are dog-friendly. Here are several options for getaways with old-fashioned appeal:

☞ Barkwells jnt.im/193, in Mills River, NC, offers seven pet-friendly cabins on a fully fenced seven-acre property within easy reach of Asheville, the Biltmore, and hiking trails in the Blue Ridge Mountains. Your dog can exercise in your cabin's fenced yard or with the other visiting dogs, and he's welcome to play in the pond — by the end of the day, you'll all be happy to curl up in front of your cabin's fireplace. Also in North Carolina is Four Paws Kingdom jnt.im/192, a "dog dedicated campground" for RVers (cabins are also available). For a B&B alternative, try Ponder Cove jnt.im/194, near Asheville.

☞ Maryland's Savage River Lodge jnt.im/191 welcomes leashed pets (cats included) all over the property except the Lodge building itself.

☞ Similar rules apply at Vermont's Mountain Top Inn & Resort jnt.im/195.

☞ In North Georgia, check out the pet-friendly cabins at Mountain Paws jnt.im/189.

☞ Dillman's Bay Resort jnt.im/190 is an old-fashioned lake resort in Wisconsin, with cabins and fishing, hiking, and boating — and art workshops too, for the creatively inclined. Dogs and cats are welcome.

☞ At the unaffordable end of the scale, The Point Resort jnt.im/188 in the Adirondacks welcomes "well-trained and well-behaved pets jnt.im/196" (see p. 24). Not far away, Lake Placid Lodge jnt.im/185, a Relais & Chateaux property, opens all but one of its cabins to "well-trained, quiet dogs;" the Lodge at Glendorn jnt.im/186, another Relais & Chateaux property in northwestern Pennsylvania, welcomes pet dogs to all of its cabins, and to the Big House's terrace and screened porch between meals.

☞ On the West Coast, check out the three Sheep Dung Properties jnt.im/184 (you know your dog will love that!) in and near Boonville, CA: All three options are dog-friendly, but the Other Place and the Long Valley Ranch offer cabins surrounded by fenced acreage, and a lot of thought jnt.im/187 for your pup's comfort. Lakedale Resort jnt.im/182 on San Juan Island, north of Seattle, allows pet dogs in its Lake House and log cabins (my niece was married there not long ago, and the place was so pretty it distracted me from the wedding).

SKILL-LEARNING VACATIONS

Why not go one step further, and take a vacation that focuses on your dog, and the fun you can have learning new skills

together? Every summer, Vermont's Camp Gone to the Dogs jnt.im/183 holds several week-long sessions teaching your dog and you all kinds of skills, including agility, swimming, tracking, herding, lure coursing, and frisbee. Join the Dog Scouts of America jnt.im/180 and go back to camp jnt.im/181 with your dog — together you'll earn badges in every conceivable dog friendly activity (while the main camp is in Michigan, "mini-camps" are held in other U.S. locations). Other options include Camp Dogwood jnt.im/178 in Ingleside, Illinois, the Canine Camp Getaway jnt.im/179 in Lake George, NY, and the "canine outdoor adventures jnt.im/177" at Glen Highland Farm, just east of New York's Finger Lakes.

I've given you a lot of suggestions, but there are more that I haven't listed, and many more that I haven't thought of (yet!). I'm not a golfer, for example, so I haven't found you dog-friendly golf courses, but I suspect they exist (in fact, I now know they do — how could I stop myself from doing a bit of research after typing that?). My hope is that these suggestions will encourage you to assume that no matter where you want to go, or what you'd like to do, there will be a way to structure your trip so that you can share it with your wonderful dog — because so often there is.

3

Digs: Finding a dog-friendly hotel

You've decided where you'd like to go, but how do find a place where you and your pet can sleep? You will find many on-line resources, leading you to a wealth of choices. You will also find, when you look closely at a hotel (or campground, or vacation rental) pet policy, that some "pet-friendly" places truly welcome pets (Kimpton hotels, for example, accept pets of all kinds and sizes, don't charge a fee, and make a fuss over your pet on arrival), while others tolerate them, charging a hefty (and non-refundable) cleaning fee and drawing the line at pets over a certain weight. To the extent you can, given your travel plans, seek out and reward with your patronage the places that make it easy for you and your pet to be together.

HOTEL CHAINS AND GROUPS

If you have a favorite hotel chain or group, and you know that its member hotels are typically pet-friendly, you might start with their site, particularly if you're trying to accumulate reward points.

On the budget end of the scale, Red Roof Inn `jnt.im/570`, Motel 6 `jnt.im/571`, La Quinta `jnt.im/569`, Candlewood Suites `jnt.im/572`, Travelodge `jnt.im/567` and Best Western `jnt.im/568` have nationwide (and, in some cases, international) networks; it seems as though you are never too far away from one of them.

Outside the U.S., the Accor Hotel Group is typically pet-friendly: Ibis `jnt.im/566` hotels are pet-friendly, for example, as are many Mercure `jnt.im/573` hotels.

You may well find a pet-friendly hotel in the mid-range chains, including Hampton Inn, Embassy Suites, Residence Inn, and Doubletree. A trendier, but still affordable, choice is the Aloft Hotel `jnt.im/564` collection. Abroad, an attractive option are the serviced Citadines Apart'Hotels `jnt.im/563`. I learned about Citadines from a Dog Jaunt reader who spent a week in one in Paris's Bastille neighborhood with her Toy Poodle "and loved it," but the chain has options around the world.

At the higher end of the spectrum, the Kimpton `jnt.im/565` hotels are delightful and genuinely pet-friendly. Your pet can also stay with you at W hotels `jnt.im/562`, Loews `jnt.im/574` hotels, Four Seasons hotels (look out for weight limits), and at many Ritz-Carlton hotels.

Regional chains and groups, including boutique-style hotel groups, also open their doors to pets. A good budget-conscious choice in the U.S.'s

Before you make your reservation at any hotel, confirm by phone, with the hotel (not a booking agency), that it is pet-friendly. Though some groups have only pet-friendly hotels, others include some hotels that aren't. Ask for details about your hotel's pet policy, so you can bring a copy of your pet's shot record, for example, if it's required. Also, print a copy of your hotel's pet policy at the time of booking, whether the information is on the hotel's website or in a confirmation e-mail, so you have it to refer to if a hotel's pet fees or policies change between the date you make your plans and the date you check in.

central and southeastern states is the Drury Hotel jnt.im/558 group. The Hotel Indigo jnt.im/559 hotels are generally pet-friendly, and while not every inn, B&B and hotel in the Unique Inns jnt.im/557 group welcomes pets, the group makes it easy for guests to identify the ones that do by putting a "pets welcome" button on its main search page (the same goes for the Coast Hotels & Resorts jnt.im/560 group).

Europe, too, is sprinkled with regional hotel groups, many of which accept pets. For example:

☞ Motel One hotels jnt.im/555, primarily in Germany but also in Austria (more coming soon in Belgium and the U.K.), are dog-friendly.

☞ Travelodge jnt.im/556 offers very basic lodging in the U.K. and Spain for very basic prices, and many locations are pet-friendly (to find out if a location you're considering is pet-friendly, either call or start filling out a booking form — a pet-friendly location will give you the option of adding your pet during the booking process).

☞ Leonardo hotels jnt.im/554, located primarily in Germany and Israel, but with locations in Austria, Switzerland, Belgium, and Hungary, are all pet-friendly.

HISTORY BUFFS AND LUXURY LOVERS

If you would prefer to stay somewhere steeped in history, a very tempting option is to rent one of the historic properties jnt.im/561 offered by the National Trust or the Landmark Trust — most are in Britain (the enchanting line-up includes cottages, towers, follies, mills, gatehouses and manor houses), but some are in

other parts of Europe (including a 16th c. Palladian villa in Vicenza, and Le Moulin de la Tuilerie, the former French home of the Duke and Duchess of Windsor). Scotland jnt.im/550 and Ireland jnt.im/100 have their own collections of gorgeous historic properties, and many of them can be visited or rented by vacationers with pets.

In the U.S., check out the Historic Hotels of America jnt.im/551, a group of over 235 "quality hotels that have faithfully maintained their historic integrity, architecture and ambiance." Many of the properties are pet-friendly, but because the website doesn't support searching by that characteristic, you'll have to look at the individual listings to find out which ones.

If you're looking for luxury as well as history, choose one of Relais & Chateaux jnt.im/549's exquisite properties or something divine from the Chateaux & Hotels jnt.im/548 collection. If you are a fan of the Small Luxury Hotels of the World group, you'll need to turn to the back (pp. 58-63) of their online "magazine jnt.im/552" and click around the listings for the destination you're interested in (SLH has a new mobile app, but it doesn't include information about pet policies). For each property, click on "Services," and then look under "On-site facilities" to see if pets are accepted (you'll need to call for the pet policy details). The properties are gorgeous, and many of them accept pets, so your time and effort won't be wasted.

USEFUL TRAVEL WEBSITES

If you aren't particularly loyal to a hotel chain or group, there are some excellent on-line resources that will help you find pet-friendly hotels, inns and campgrounds:

☞ Unlike other sites, which merely tell you whether a property is pet-friendly or not, Go Pet Friendly jnt.im/545 provides details about a property's pet policy — which is useful for everyone, but particularly for travelers with non-canine pets, multiple pets, or large dogs. (The site, which focuses on travel in the U.S. and Canada, also offers travelers with pets a drawer full of other useful tools, including the Road Trip Planner jnt.im/546: Tell it where you want to go, and what you'll need along the way, and it will generate a map showing pet-friendly hotels, campgrounds, restaurants, activities and services along the way. Click on the ones you want to add them as destinations, then click "View Itinerary." You'll be given a set of road directions for your trip.) Another favorite is Bring Fido jnt.im/544, which lists dog-friendly hotels, restaurants and attractions worldwide.

☞ I also rely heavily on TripAdvisor jnt.im/547, especially for trips outside the U.S. On the main search page, make sure "Hotels" is checked, and type in your destination. On the resulting page, scroll down until you see, in the sidebar on the left, the "Amenities" list. Click on "Pets Allowed," and you'll get a shorter list of hotels, ranked in order of popularity with travelers. You will need to do your own research about the particulars of each property's pet policy.

☞ In Britain and Ireland (as well as France, Italy, Portugal and Spain), the Alastair Sawday's jnt.im/542 site is a way to find delightful pet-friendly hotels, rentals and luxury camping opportunities.

Click on "Map" in the menu bar, zoom to the region or country you're interested in, and check the "Pets welcome" box (along with any other features you're seeking). The resulting map will be dotted with properties that meet your criteria — click on each to check them out in detail.

☞ If you're traveling in Australia, check out Holidaying with Dogs jnt.im/543 and Take a Break (which has a section devoted to pet-friendly accommodations jnt.im/553). Travel Dog Australia jnt.im/539, written by a blogger traveling with her dogs Chilly and Max, offers information about affordable (preferably free!) dog-friendly camping. In New Zealand, I'd start with the AA jnt.im/540's list of pet-friendly hotels (U.S. travelers will recognize the practical, reliable AAA travel brand, even without the third "A").

VACATION RENTALS

HomeAway and VRBO are good resources jnt.im/538 for international pet-friendly rentals at reasonable prices, and so is FlipKey jnt.im/541 (once you have an initial list of search results, check the "Pet friendly" box, under "Amenities"). Non-U.S. companies include Holidays jnt.im/536, especially useful for vacation rentals in the U.K. and France (on the main page, click on "Multi-criteria search" and check the "Pets allowed" box), and the Alastair Sawday's jnt.im/537 site mentioned earlier. Take a look, too, at France's Gites de France jnt.im/534, which offers not only rural retreats but also in-city rentals — and for a modest price.

You will find shoals of city- and country-focused rental agencies representing owners of rental properties, but be prepared to learn jnt.im/535 that their listings are not available to travelers with pets. If you persevere, you'll succeed: Make a phone call for your initial contact, rather than sending an e-mail or filling out an agency's on-line form, and follow up with an e-mail that includes a picture of your pet (looking as charming and small as possible) and whatever assurances you can honestly give about your pet's good guest behavior (*e.g.,* he's house-trained and quiet, you travel with a crate as well as sheets for the furniture).

Peer-to-peer rentals jnt.im/533 may be pet-friendly, but it's often difficult to find out. The companies that make it easiest for travelers with pets are Roomorama, Wimdu and Airbnb.

HOTEL AND HOUSE GUEST ETIQUETTE AND SAFETY

Whether you're staying in a hotel or in a friend's guest room, you'll want to let your host know ahead of time you'll be visiting with a pet, and you'll want to ensure that your pet arrives clean and free of fleas. Those are both basic necessities; here are some suggestions for making the visit a success:

➤ If you need to bathe your pet while you're there (and you will — Chloe has required at least one bath on every trip we've taken with her), use your own towels — bring a supply of quick-drying microfiber towels with you — and pack a hair stopper to put over the bathtub's drain.
➤ Pack at least two sheets that you can use to cover your bed and the piece

of furniture — a sofa or armchair — your pet is most likely to head for.
➤ If you have a crate for your pet, set it up in your room, so it's out of the way, and feed your pet there too (bring your own food and water bowls with you, and wash the food bowl after each meal, so crumbs don't attract ants).
➤ Unless you have complete confidence in your dog's house training, keep him near you (on a leash, if necessary). Take him outside more often than you would at home, to be on the safe side.
➤ Bring a bottle of enzymatic cleaner with you, and respond promptly to accidents.
➤ And remember this basic truth: A tired pet is a good guest.

At the same time, you'll want to think about hazards for your pet in your hotel room or your host's house. You will know best what temptations your pet can't resist. Here are some tips we've picked up over the years:

➤ If your dog chews on cords, pack a roll of blue painter's tape (it'll release easily when you want it to, and won't leave the cords sticky) and secure dangling or trailing cords out of your pet's reach.
➤ If he finds small objects irresistible, scan your hotel room for the TV remote, or for toiletries left on the bathtub's edge, and put them out of reach. Ask your host to help you keep his child's Lego collection behind a closed door (look out, too, for chess pieces and foam darts).
➤ If your pet finds the distinction between pee pads and throw rugs murky, roll up the throw rugs and stow them

out of harm's way (and be vigilant about picking up your bath mat).

➤ If your pet is likely to walk out an open door, keep him leashed — a family that's used to being casual about entering and exiting cannot be expected to suddenly change its habits.

➤ Hosts who don't have a pet themselves will not know about food hazards like chocolate, grapes/raisins, macadamia nuts, and any product containing Xylitol, which can be fatal for pets (avocado and cooked bones are also dangerous) — again, if you keep your pet leashed, or near you, you are less likely to find him being given an inappropriate treat by a well-meaning friend.

More and more hotels, inns, and vacation rentals are opening their doors to pets. Pet guests cause relatively little trouble, many managers have pointed out (you hardly ever hear of a dog stealing towels, or getting drunk and partying until all hours), and their owners are a welcome source of business. With just a little digging, you and your pup will find a perfect place to spend the night — or a week!

4

Bone appetit: Finding dog-friendly restaurants

The question of whether pet dogs should be allowed to join their owners for a meal is as contentious as any you'll ever encounter. On one side of the argument are people concerned about dog bites, unsanitary messes, and allergies; on the other are pet owners who regard their dogs as civilized companions, and the restaurant owners and managers who wish to cater to them.

Speaking generally, the situation in the U.S. is difficult for dog owners, but more and more jurisdictions are allowing pet dogs to keep their owners company at outdoor patio tables. That process is only starting in Australia, and hasn't started at all in New Zealand. Europe is a happier place for hungry travelers with pets; though the locals may feel attitudes are cooling, a visitor from the U.S. basks in the unaccustomed warmth.

FINDING A DOG-FRIENDLY U.S. RESTAURANT

The U.S. Food and Drug Administration recommends that animals, with some exceptions, none of which include pets dogs, be prohibited from retail establishments where food is served (FDA code provision 6-501.115 jnt.im/530). It is up to

Call ahead and ask if your dog can join you at an outside table. Even better, walk up and inquire in person. The sight of your clean and charming pup may tip the balance in your favor.

the states to implement laws regarding pets in restaurants, and the states have followed the FDA's recommendation, with some variations jnt.im/531 (e.g., some states are open to variances or local ordinances that permit dogs — and it generally is dogs, not cats or other pets — in outdoor eating areas).

What that means for you is that in some states or cities you can find restaurants with outdoor patios that officially welcome diners with pet dogs, but in many you can't (complicating the picture, some restaurants in pet-unfriendly jurisdictions will turn a blind eye to diners with pets, hoping that overworked health inspectors will not notice violations). If you are planning a trip with your dog, do some quick research about the cities and counties you'll be visiting. Remember that even in favorable jurisdictions, it's up to the restaurant to take advantage of the option.

Currently, restaurants in Maryland jnt.im/529 may choose to open their patios to diners with pet dogs. In other states (Florida and California are leading the way, but the movement appears to be nationwide), counties and cities have won or are seeking to give restaurant owners the same options.

Go Pet Friendly jnt.im/175 and PetFriendlyTravel.com jnt.im/176 will point you to dog-friendly restaurants in the U.S. and Canada, and Bring Fido jnt.im/174 has worldwide listings.

Recent successes include <u>Los Angeles County</u> jnt.im/528 (except for the cities of Pasadena, Long Beach and Vernon, which have their own rules), <u>Houston</u> jnt.im/532, and <u>Arlington, VA</u> jnt.im/526. The legal landscape changes nearly every month.

Fail-proof alternatives are drive-through restaurants, or the 50's-style drive-ins that let you park and eat in your car. In big cities, seek out food trucks, which have <u>come a long way</u> jnt.im/527 from the hot dog carts you remember from childhood visits to New York. In <u>Portland, OR</u> jnt.im/523, there are so many food trucks that they've clumped together into "pods," and are a crucial part of the amazing local food scene. If you're visiting New York City, I recommend following the Twitter feed of <u>@nycfoodtruck</u> jnt.im/524 for updates on food truck locations and specials. Elsewhere, a Google search for "[city you're visiting] food truck" will lead you to sites with local food truck listings and locations.

EATING WITH YOUR DOG IN EUROPE

Traditionally, restaurants in certain European countries, especially France and Italy, have been very welcoming. That attitude may be cooling, but it is still certainly easier to dine (or at least lunch) with your pup in Paris than in Chicago. Britain has a reputation for pet-friendliness that <u>it may not deserve</u> jnt.im/521, but you can still find a dog-friendly pub for your Ploughman's Lunch.

There are few on-line resources for dog-friendly European restaurants. Bring Fido has a few listings for major cities, but generally speaking, you're on your own. Your best approach is to ask in person, since your friendly and well-mannered pup will likely be his own best advocate. It is more likely that your dog will be welcome for coffee or a drink at an outside table or in a bar, or lunch in a bistro, than in a fancy restaurant for dinner. There's no harm in asking, however, and you may be pleasantly surprised. Be polite, and express happiness and gratitude when your request is granted (and only disappointment if it is denied — in Paris, a sorrowful "Dommage!" will cover it).

Food carts are starting to catch on in Europe, and look for take-away counters. Some of the best falafel you'll ever have is available at L'As du Fallafel's walk-up counter in Paris's Marais neighborhood, and the city is sprinkled with walk-up crêpe counters. You will also be able to pick up cooked food (as well as groceries) at one of Paris's many outdoor markets.

The same <u>Alastair Sawday's</u> jnt.im/522 site you consulted for dog-friendly hotels and inns in the U.K. and parts of Europe will also direct you to <u>dog-friendly British pubs</u> jnt.im/520. Other useful resources are <u>Doggie Pubs</u> jnt.im/525 and <u>Dog Friendly Britain</u> jnt.im/518, both with good coverage in England, Scotland and Wales. Be sure to confirm that an establishment still welcomes dogs, in case their policy has recently changed.

EATING WITH YOUR DOG DOWN UNDER

When I wrote this section last year, Australia prohibited pets from all eating areas, including beer gardens and patios. A recent change in Australia New Zealand Food Standards Code, <u>Standard 3.2.2</u> jnt.im/519 now means, however, that "A food business may permit a dog that is not an assistance animal to be present in an outdoor dining area" (where "outdoor dining area" is defined as "an area that is used for dining, drinking or both drinking and dining; and is not used for the preparation of food; and is not an enclosed area; and can be entered by the public without passing through an enclosed area"). That paves the way for local councils to pass supportive bylaws, which is just starting to happen (*e.g.*, in Sunshine Coast jnt.im/516, just north of Brisbane).

Despite the code's name, Standard 3.2.2 does not apply in New Zealand, which hasn't yet seen the light: "Every occupier of food premises," says New Zealand's Food Hygiene Regulations 1974 (Part 2, Section 11 jnt.im/517), "shall ensure that no animal is permitted on the premises" other than service animals and cats "suppress[ing] rodents."

RESTAURANT PETIQUETTE

While you may encounter servers who turn to mush over your dog (one waiter at Paris's Au Pied de Cochon — a haven for victims of jetlag, since it serves French onion soup around the clock — followed Chloe outside to give her a champagne cork to play with), you shouldn't expect it. Your goal is to validate the restaurant's decision to take a chance on your dog by ensuring that he is a good guest:

➤ Locals may put their dog on a seat, but you should guide yours under the table and settle him into a comfortable down position (reinforce it with a foot on his leash, encouraging him to keep his head down).
➤ Tie or loop the end of his leash around your chair leg, or sit on its handle end, in case your foot shifts during the meal.

➤ If you walked for a while before entering the restaurant, your job will be much easier — he'll be ready for a nap. Just in case, though, bring along a chew that you can give him if he seems bored or overly interested in your food.
➤ Do not feed him scraps from your plate, and do not put your plate down for him to lick.
➤ Prevent him from approaching other diners, unless they expressly invite him to (and even then, keep the meeting brief).
➤ A perfectly successful meal with your dog is one where the neighboring table is surprised to see him emerge at the end of the meal. If he gets praise and attention at that point, he (and you) will have earned it. As you depart, make an effort to thank the person who admitted you.

Things are looking up for hungry travelers with pets (and for restaurant owners who would like to have the option of attracting their business). In a pinch, though, think outside the (lunch)box and find a drive-through, a walk-up counter, a food truck — or pack a picnic. Why should your dog be the only one to lie down during a meal?

5

Ruff road: Driving with your pet

A road trip that starts in your own driveway is a straightforward way to travel with your pet (assuming, of course, that she's not prone to motion sickness). Packing is easy — toss your stuff and your pet's stuff in totes, and go. That said, there's a short list of things you'll want to do to make sure your pet is safe and comfortable on the road.

KEEPING YOUR PET SAFE IN THE CAR

You'll see small dogs sitting on their owner's laps, and big dogs with their heads out the window, but neither is a good idea. In an accident, your unrestrained pet becomes a missile. She'll be injured or killed, and she'll pose a serious threat to you as well. Hawaii jnt.im/513 has a law that prevents pets from traveling on a driver's lap, or elsewhere in the car's cabin, and several other states jnt.im/514 are using rules against distracted driving and improper animal transport to clamp down on lap pets. New Jersey is considering a pet "seat belt" law, and my guess is that the trend will continue.

This section describes options for keeping your pet secure, as

Do not attach the car safety belt to your pet's collar; in a collision, a harness will distribute pressure over your pet's chest, instead of focusing it on her neck.

well as other car safety issues you may not have considered.

SECURING YOUR SMALL DOG

When I first wrote this section, my top pick for a car safety solution was the one Chloe was using: A padded booster seat combined with a harness and safety belt. It gave Chloe a view out the window while keeping her securely clipped to our car's frame. Last year, however, the Center for Pet Safety caught everyone's attention with a series of videos jnt.im/512 showing what happens to a crash-test dummy of a Boxer wearing a number of safety harnesses/tethers (makers unidentified) in a 30 mph crash. I was so horrified by the videos that I immediately disposed of Chloe's harness and tether and Snoozer booster seat.

What we use now is the Pet Tube jnt.im/511 from Pet Ego, a lightweight car kennel that hooks over one or more car seat headrests. It comes in two sizes; the larger can occupy the entire back seat, or only a portion of it, as you prefer. We use the small size for Chloe, and it would work for dogs even larger than she is – say up to 20 lbs. I like it because it provides her with a lot of room and ventilation, but unlike a crate, lets her keep an eye on me (even though she can no longer look out the window). The "optional" Comfort Pillow is pretty much necessary; it gives your pet a firm, flat surface to rest on (you'll need to add a soft crate pad before it's really comfortable, though). I also like it because it collapses to a 3″ × 18″ pancake that can, along with the Comfort Pillow, be packed in Chloe's suitcase, if we plan to drive once we arrive at our destination.

A hard-sided crate is the safest choice, however. The classic option, used extensively by dog show professionals, is the PetMate Sky Kennel you'll hear more about later in the book, when you're considering air travel. If Chloe weighed less than 10 lbs., I'd take a good look at the Penthouse jnt.im/510 from 4pets, a Swiss company, which promises to give her the protection of a hard-sided crate but with the window view of her old booster seat.

If I can't talk you out of the booster seat option, choose one that can be securely strapped to the car with a seat belt, like the L.A. Rider Seat jnt.im/509. Position it in the right rear passenger seat, so you can see and reach your dog (the front passenger seat is a bad choice unless you disable the air bag). Buy a well-padded and well-made harness and a safety belt with a clip that attaches to one of your car's latch bars (my choices for Chloe were the Canine Friendly Vest Harness jnt.im/515 and the PetBuckle Kwik-Connect Tether jnt.im/506).

I'm hearing good things about Sleepypod's new Clickit Utility harness jnt.im/507), but it looks like it will not work with a booster seat. Instead, put a pad or a towel or a dog bed on the back seat of your car for your pup to lie on.

A bird will do well in one of the Celltei Pak-o-Bird jnt.im/104 carriers. If yours is a chewer, she might do better in a Wingabago jnt.im/105 carrier (be careful to monitor her temperature, since the carriers hold heat and cold) or the sturdy King's Cages jnt.im/103 travel carrier. Secure the latter two by passing your car's seatbelt around them; the Pak-o-Bird carriers have loops on their backs through which the seatbelt can be passed.

SECURING A BIG DOG IN A CAR

Bigger dogs will do best in a crate that is tethered to the tie-downs in the back of your car. Again, the PetMate Sky Kennel is the gold standard of hard-sided crates, but the ProLine jnt.im/505 crate from 4pets is an exciting new option. Alternatively, your car may have a grate accessory that blocks off the rear area, turning it into a large crate. Think about the volume of space you allow your dog, though — the area she's given to roam around in will, in an accident, also be the space she's tossed around in.

While there are car safety options for big dogs that include a harness and safety belt (a larger version of the small dog solution), or a harness attached to a "zip line jnt.im/504" that extends sideways across your car's back seat, I no longer feel good about any of them after seeing that crash test video. The Sleepypod harness I mentioned earlier may change my mind.

ADDITIONAL PET SAFETY CONCERNS

However your dog is secured while you're rolling down the highway, when you stop be sure to attach her leash before you open the car door, even if she can be counted on to stay near you. An unexpected and startling sound (real life examples include train whistles and truck horns) may send her from your side in a panic.

Other safety issues include eye protection (an open window is a dog's joy, but also the source of eye damage from road grit and wind — either buy a screen for your window jnt.im/503, or goggles jnt.im/508 for your dog) and temperature control. Even when you're in the car together, your pet may be in direct sun while you're comfortably shaded.

Keep an eye on her, and put up a window shade jnt.im/500 if she's showing signs of discomfort. In a pinch, you can close your car's side window on a towel or a t-shirt to block the sun, but a purchased shade is see-through, so safer for driving.

It is always risky to leave your pet in your car. In many jurisdictions, it's illegal. Even in mild weather, your car will heat up extraordinarily quickly to temperatures your pet cannot handle, and in cold weather, your car will function like a refrigerator jnt.im/501. Cracking a window will not solve the problem, and will, moreover, make it easier for someone to steal your pet.

The main reasons you'd consider leaving your pet behind are bathroom breaks and meals. If you're traveling with a companion, take bathroom breaks in turns, if you're on your own, deploy your stealth bag or, if you have a big dog, seek out rest areas and bring your buddy in

If you're traveling with a cat, stop every so often to give her a chance at her litter box. Options for a traveling litter box include a stack of disposable cardboard litter boxes jnt.im/491 or Kitty Kan boxes jnt.im/492 (they're enclosed, to reduce litter tracking and flinging), or one of a number of collapsible options. The Go Kitty Go box jnt.im/489 can be reused and, ultimately, recycled, while the 2-gallon SturdiBox jnt.im/490 can be reused indefinitely (wipe it and the Go Kitty Go box out with cleaning wipes to keep them fresh on the road; at home, wash them with detergent). For all of the options other than the Kitty Kan (which includes litter), bring a resealable zippered storage bag of litter from your cat's home box to assure her that this new litter box is to be trusted.

with you, as rapidly and discreetly as possible. With a little planning, research and creativity, you can remain with your dog at mealtime too. Find a restaurant that allows your pet to join you (on a patio or other outdoor seating, in the U.S.), eat at drive-through restaurants, or have a picnic.

MAKING A CAR TRIP COMFORTABLE

If your pet is secured with a harness and seat belt rather than a crate (or the crate-like Pet Tube), drape a sheet or towel over your car's back seat, to protect your pet from a hot surface and to protect your seat from her fur and drool. If it's going to

The stealth bag we use for Chloe is the large Contour Messenger Bag jnt.im/493 from Pet Ego, which will comfortably hold a dog up to 15 lbs. A smaller dog (say, under 10 lbs.) will fit in the small size. You may be wondering how the same person who disapproves of fake service animal vests can justify sneaking a dog into a convenience store bathroom. To me, the latter misbehavior is simpler and less far-reaching in its effects. By sneaking, I am not injuring the cause of service animal owners, who urgently need to have their relationship with their companions recognized and respected. At most, I am risking causing another person allergy problems, though a dog entirely contained in a carrier is extremely unlikely to be a source of trouble (I am also risking the embarrassment of being caught and asked to leave, but that only harms me). To minimize even that potential effect, I seldom sneak, and only in places I can leave immediately, if asked to.

As you might have guessed, this is another of those instances where Frommer's and I parted ways. While I am ordinarily law-abiding, I will not leave a dog in a car under any circumstances.

be a long trip, you might invest in a car seat protector jnt.im/502 that clips around your car's headrests and provides protection for the vertical part of your seat cushions. Bring a pad, or even your pet's regular bed, for your pet to snooze on. Bring a favorite toy, and fill a Kong chew toy every so often to keep her entertained. Stop every couple of hours and let her stretch her legs, use the bathroom and have a drink of water.

PET-FRIENDLY CAR RENTALS AND SHARES

What if you fly somewhere and then rent a car? First of all, remember to pack a car safety solution. A small pet could travel in the same in-cabin carrier you used for plane travel, but if I know we'll be driving a lot at our destination, I carry Chloe's Pet Tube and not-so-optional comfort pillow with us.

Several of the biggest U.S. car rental companies (Advantage, Alamo, Avis, Budget, Hertz, National) have pet policies jnt.im/499 on their web sites. Put briefly, pets are allowed, but you will be charged if extra cleaning is required. These companies also rent abroad. If you are renting from a company based outside the U.S., search their "Terms & Conditions" page (Europcar jnt.im/497, for example, allows the transportation of domestic animals "subject to prior authorisation by Europcar") or contact them directly for their pet policy.

How about car-share companies like Zipcar? Most allow pets jnt.im/496 in their cars if they are fully contained in a carrier. If you are not near a Zipcar (the company currently has locations in the U.S., Canada and the U.K.), or if you want to check out a local alternative, CarSharing.net jnt.im/498 is a valuable resource.

Contact the company you're interested in to find out about its pet policy.

Reduce the chance that you will be charged for extra cleaning by carrying a seat cover with you, or at least a sheet or towel you can drape and tuck to protect the upholstery. Use a lint roller before you return the car to the rental agency, and wipe nose prints off the windows with a packet of Windex wipes.

TRAVELING IN AN RV WITH A PET

If you own an RV (or caravan), you either have a pet yourself or you know an RVer who does. One of the joys of being an RV owner is that your pet (and often more than one pet!) can travel with you. It's particularly pleasant for owners of large dogs to travel without worrying about finding a hotel that welcomes pets bigger than a breadbox.

Even in a vehicle that looks and feels like a small apartment, you'll need to think about your pet's safety and comfort:

➤ Use a crate for your dog, or a harness plus safety belt secured to the safety belt or frame of your RV's sofa.

➤ If you are pulling a trailer, keep your pet with you in the cab of your truck.

➤ If you must carry one or more pets behind you, crate them (with plenty of bedding for padding) and ensure that the crate is firmly secured to the floor or a wall of the trailer. Make sure that the trailer's air-conditioning system is working properly. Stop frequently to check on your pet, and to give her a chance to stretch her legs. An excellent resource for RVers with pets is Woodall's Camping and RVing with Dogs jnt.im/495, which suggests that you use a baby monitor to keep an eye on a pet in a towed trailer, between stops.

➤ An RV will heat up just like a car, even on a seemingly mild day, so if you must leave your pet, be sure that your RV's air-conditioning is working. What if the A/C stops working, or the campground's power fails? Have a back-up, and a second back-up, in place. Solutions include monitors that, triggered by temperature changes, notify you and start a ventilating fan or the RV's power generator.

➤ Consider leaving your contact info with your neighbors, so you can be reached easily if a need arises for you to return.

Be considerate of your campground neighbors (and protect your dog, too) by keeping your pup leashed. A small dog can be contained (and given some room to play) in a collapsible exercise pen jnt.im/494; for her safety, stay near her while she's in the pen. Don't leave your pet behind if you know that some noise at this particular campground sets off your pup's bark response. As a kindness to your pup, give her a long walk before you leave, so she'll doze in your absence.

Several RV companies in the U.S. (*e.g.,* Cruise America, Camping World) and abroad (*e.g.,* Abacus and Just Go, in the U.K.), will rent vehicles to pet owners. Remember to pack a car safety solution for your pet. Since you don't know how well your rented camper's air conditioning will work, or how reliable the back-up systems are (if they exist), you should plan not to leave your pet in the camper.

Driving with your dog has been a joy since the first time a dog hopped into her owner's horseless carriage. There are more horseless carriages on the road now than there were then, and they travel faster (and farther) now, so make sure your pup is safe and comfortable before you leave the driveway. With just a bit of planning and a few pieces of gear, you'll both rule the road.

While you won't have to find a pet-friendly hotel, you will have to find a pet-friendly campground. Go Pet Friendly is a great resource (on the main page, click on "Search by Category," and then on "Campgrounds" to start your search). Be warned: As with hotels, some campgrounds are more pet tolerant than pet friendly.

Companies renting RVs to pet owners will either charge a fee if extra cleaning is needed (*e.g.,* Cruise America) or take a pet deposit up front. In either case, the penalty for a dirty RV is substantial enough that you'll want to clean up your rental before you return it (pack or purchase lint rollers, Windex wipes, and cleaning wipes).

6

Bus, train, and boat

I t's difficult to summarize the rules you'll encounter regarding pets on buses, trains, and boats, because they vary by country and by region, by type of transportation and by kind of pet. The good news is that if you have a pet (especially a dog) small enough to fit in a carrier, you can bring her with you on many public transit systems, and she'll be welcome on nearly every European train. This section highlights some of the available (and unavailable) options. Use these suggestions to start creating an itinerary of your own, whether you're planning an odyssey or day trips from a fixed base.

BARK OF THE BUS: TRAVELING BY COACH WITH YOUR PET

Generally speaking, the bigger bus companies (traveling interstate or between provinces in the U.S. and Canada, and internationally in Europe) do not allow pets on board. Smaller or regional bus lines may allow pets on board, but typically only small animals in carriers. Public transit buses often do allow pets on board; on occasion, large pets are allowed.

INTER-CITY BUSES

The big inter-city bus lines serving the U.S. and Canada (Greyhound, Megabus, BoltBus, Peter Pan, Orléans Express) do not allow pets on board jnt.im/484. Trailways leaves the decision to its constituent companies, which haven't welcomed pets either.

Similarly, in Europe, Euroline's buses do not allow pets on board, with rare exceptions (*e.g.,* Hungary's Vola'nbusz opens the door to small pets in carriers jnt.im/482, but only on the Budapest-Wien and Budapest-Subotica lines, and for a 50% one-way fare each way). Another exception is the Czech Republic's Student Agency buses jnt.im/483, which travel between Prague or Budapest and destinations all over Europe, and allow small pets in carriers on board.

Greyhound Australia jnt.im/481 only allows service animals onboard, and the same is true for New Zealand's InterCity Coachlines jnt.im/485 and NakedBus.com jnt.im/479.

REGIONAL BUSES

The story improves when you look at regional bus lines. In the U.S., for example, the Hampton Jitney jnt.im/480 (serving Long Island and New England) allows small pets in carriers on board, as does Oregon's Breeze Bus jnt.im/477.

In Switzerland, the PostBus jnt.im/478 welcomes small animals in carriers and large dogs if muzzled and on a short leash. Scottish CityLink jnt.im/476 will let you travel with your small pet in a carrier, under your feet. While it will take a little digging in some cases (look under a site's FAQ section, "terms of carriage" or "conditions of carriage" to find out whether animals are permitted), you and your budget may be pleasantly surprised by what you find.

PUBLIC TRANSIT BUSES

Public transit buses jnt.im/486 are, more
often than not, pet-friendly (*i.e.*, small
pets in lap-sized carriers are allowed
onboard). A few public transit systems in
the U.S. even accept leashed big dogs (*e.g.*,
Seattle's buses, monorail and light rail,
New York's Metro-North trains). There
are exceptions, like Austin's public transit,
and the Bay Area's CalTrain trains, so you
can't assume your pet will be welcome.

Pets of all sizes, either leashed
or in a carrier, are allowed on buses
in London jnt.im/473 (as well as the
Emirates Air Line, a gondola line
crossing the Thames), Berlin jnt.im/474,
Calgary jnt.im/471, Toronto jnt.im/472
(during non-peak hours), and possibly
Dublin jnt.im/470. Small pets in carriers
can travel on buses in Paris jnt.im/475,
Vancouver jnt.im/468, Montreal jnt.im/469,
and Quebec jnt.im/467 (see Section
3) — but not Ottawa jnt.im/487.

In the land of Oz, small pets in carriers
can travel on buses in Sydney jnt.im/463
and Melbourne jnt.im/464, but not
Brisbane jnt.im/462, Perth jnt.im/465,
Hobart, or Alice Springs jnt.im/461.

The bigger bus lines will likely disap-
point you, but as you tighten your focus,
the picture improves: Some regional bus
lines allow small pets in carriers on board;
and sniff around a city's transportation
page (or call the contact number) — you
may well find that you and your pet will
be able to forego taxis and rented cars.

MAKING TRACKS: TRAVELING BY TRAIN WITH YOUR PET

Pets are not allowed onboard the national
rail service providers in the U.S., Australia
and New Zealand, and they might just as

well be barred from Canada's VIA Rail,
given the restrictions on their carriage.
The situation is considerably better when
you look at smaller, and especially public
transit, train systems, and it's downright
great when you look at Europe.

IN THE U.S.

While pet dogs used to be allowed on
board Amtrak trains, that policy was
changed in 1976 jnt.im/459. Now only
service animals jnt.im/460 are allowed on
board. Some regional carriers make it
possible (though not attractive) to travel
with your pet: The Alaska Railroad Corpo-
ration jnt.im/458, for example, lets your pet
travel in "an airline-approved kennel" in
the baggage car, which is neither heated
nor air-conditioned. If you're traveling
with a pet, the best current train options
in the U.S. are commuter trains and
public-transit trains — which sounds
limited, but can be very useful indeed.

For example, if you dread driving
in Manhattan, leave your car well
outside the city and take a Metro-
North jnt.im/457 train. If you have a small
pet in a carrier, you can travel together
on a host of NYC-area commuter rail
lines jnt.im/466, including Shore Line
East trains, NJ Transit trains and PATH
trains, and on the Long Island Railroad
(LIRR). You could, in fact, leave your
car in Philadelphia jnt.im/454, since
SEPTA and PATCO trains will connect
you to the NJ Transit system.

IN CANADA

In Canada, the situation is slightly
different. Pets (cats, dogs and "small
rodents" only) are allowed on VIA
Rail jnt.im/455 trains — but they must

travel in crates in the baggage car, which may be heated but won't be air-conditioned, "so your pet may be exposed to high temperatures." On long-haul trips, you may "occasionally visit and tend to your animal during the voyage when you are accompanied by a VIA Rail employee." How about the regional carriers?

- ☞ Rocky Mountaineer `jnt.im/453` does not allow pets on board.
- ☞ Ontario Northland's Polar Bear Express `jnt.im/456`, traveling between Moosonee and Cochrane, does, but it's a dubious proposition: Your pet, in his carrier, will be locked in the baggage car for the duration of the 5-hour trip (no visits allowed, and the Polar Bear Express is notorious for being delayed).
- ☞ Algoma Central `jnt.im/451` does allow pets on board, but only crated or leashed in the baggage car. Since pets are not allowed out of the baggage car at stops (unless they're leaving the train), it would not be workable to take the long tours Algoma offers, much less the 2-day "milk train" from Sault Ste. Marie to Hearst and back. However, depending on the weather, and the dog, it might be a way for you to take short trips between the vacation lodges (fishing, hunting and skiing) situated along the line.

That leaves us looking at commuter and public transit trains, where the results are more positive than not. Small pets in carriers are allowed on Vancouver `jnt.im/452`'s SkyTrain light rail and West Coast Express commuter line; on Toronto `jnt.im/450`'s subway, rapid transit trains, and streetcars,

but only during weekday off-peak hours; and on Montreal `jnt.im/488`'s metro. However, pets are *not* allowed on Ottawa's O-train (or on any of the city's other public transit options).

IN EUROPE

Europe, by contrast, is served by a wealth of pet-friendly trains. Typically, your pet will be welcome either leashed or in a carrier, and may share a sleeping car with you if you reserve an entire compartment. There are variations and exceptions (pets are not allowed on the Eurostar `jnt.im/446` trains, for example, though your pet can travel with you in your car on the Euro tunnel Le Shuttle), so do your research ahead of time, and be sure to bring a soft muzzle with you, in case that's required.

Europe's regional and public transit trains also typically allow pets on board:

- ☞ London `jnt.im/444`'s subway trains are very pet-friendly, as are its Docklands Light Railway and Tramlink systems, and its London Overground commuter rail system.
- ☞ Small pets in carriers are allowed on Paris `jnt.im/445`'s subway cars, but larger dogs, leashed and muzzled, may travel on the RER trains.

An invaluable place to start is Seat 61 `jnt.im/172`, an overview of world train travel, and particularly its page on taking your dog or pet by train `jnt.im/173`. Be sure, though, to double-check the information you get from the site with the railway companies you're considering. Norway `jnt.im/171`, for example, now allows leashed dogs and small pets on board NSB trains (though not in sleeping compartments).

☞ In Italy `jnt.im/443`, small pets in carriers may travel on national *and* regional trains; leashed and muzzled dogs can too, but with a caveat for rush hour on Mondays to Fridays. Pet dogs are allowed on Rome `jnt.im/447`'s metro (and on its buses), but full fare is required, along with a leash and muzzle.

☞ On Irish Rail `jnt.im/440`, a small pet (either leashed or in a carrier) may travel on intercity, commuter or DART trains, but a large dog may only travel, leashed and muzzled, in a Guard's Van — which effectively means that a large dog may only travel on the Dublin/Cork and Dublin/Belfast trains.

☞ On all of Spain `jnt.im/441`'s Renfe lines, only small pets in carriers are allowed on board, and the same is true of Madrid `jnt.im/438`'s subway trains.

Since the link for Rome's public transit pet policy takes you to a document you cannot highlight and copy just a bit of, here's a rough translation of Article 23 (The transport of animals):

➤ Small and medium-sized dogs are on board upon payment of a regular fare ticket. Only guide dogs accompanying the blind are eligible for free transport.

➤ All dogs — a maximum of two per car — must have a leash and muzzle, and must be sufficiently clean. Enter through the back end of the vehicle, and travel in the first and last subway car.

➤ Cats, birds and small animals may travel, for the price of a regular fare ticket, in cages or baskets no larger than 25x45x80 cm.

➤ Travelers with pets are required to pay compensation for any damage caused to persons, vehicles or property.

As you can see from these examples and links, most major transit systems either have a section on their website that talks about traveling with animals (look for FAQs, or rules for riders), or their site includes a link to their general Conditions of Carriage document. And if all else fails, call their contact number to learn their pet policy (in my experience, e-mail queries are seldom answered).

DOWN UNDER

None of the major railway companies in Australia (Queensland Rail `jnt.im/439`, CountryLink `jnt.im/437`, Great Southern Rail `jnt.im/442`) allows pets on board, nor are pets allowed on Western Australia's Transwa `jnt.im/435` line between Perth and Kalgoorie. Small pets in carriers may travel on Victoria `jnt.im/436`'s V/Line trains (not the V/Line buses), but only in the luggage car or in the luggage area of the passenger cabin (depending on the train).

Some public transit trains allow pets on board, including Melbourne `jnt.im/434`'s Metro trains. Small pets in carriers are allowed onboard Adelaide `jnt.im/448`'s Metro; larger pets are allowed onboard Sydney `jnt.im/430`'s Metro light rail and monorail at the conductor's discretion and if the pet is leashed, or, if small, in a carrier. No pets are allowed on public transit trains in Brisbane `jnt.im/431` or Perth `jnt.im/429`.

The situation is worse in New Zealand. The major carrier, KiwiRail `jnt.im/432`, does not allow pets on board, nor do Auckland's MAXX `jnt.im/428` trains and Wellington's Tranz Metro `jnt.im/433` trains. The picturesque Taieri Gorge Railway will allow your pet on board if she's small and in a carrier, and may allow your leashed dog on board (some customers

Are there any alternatives? The bus situation is grim, and the plane situation is no better. Virgin Australia jnt.im/170 only allows pets to travel as cargo; Qantas jnt.im/168 allows them to travel as checked baggage; Air New Zealand jnt.im/169 lets you choose between checked and cargo; and Jetstar jnt.im/166 and Tiger Airways jnt.im/167 only allow service animals onboard. While you may get lucky with a regional carrier, the obvious choices do not allow pets to travel in-cabin

Car rental remains an option, and if your budget is tight (and your schedule is loose), you might consider volunteering to do car relocation for a company like TransferCar jnt.im/165 (the company representative who contacted me was well aware that my blog is about traveling with a dog, so the vehicles should be dog-friendly).

don't like having pets on the train, so they're cautious about their approach).

The Pets on Trains Act of 2013 jnt.im/427 may get pets back (in a limited way) onto Amtrak trains, but there's no indication that pets will be welcome anytime soon on the national rail lines in Canada, Australia, or New Zealand. Look to regional and, especially, commuter trains for pet-friendly service in those regions. In Europe, it's a whole different story: Trains go where you want to go, they're affordable, and your pup is more likely than not to be a welcome paw-senger.

POOP DECK: SAILING WITH YOUR PET

This section touches on a whole range of cruising options, from glamorous ocean liners (well, *one* glamorous ocean liner) to ferries to private sailboats.

TRAVELING BY SHIP

The glamorous ocean liner is the Queen Mary 2, which is the only major cruise ship to allow pets on board. Kennel service jnt.im/425 is available on all crossings between Southampton and New York City. Twelve kennels are available, and the pets also have access to an indoor playroom and an outdoor deck. A kennel master looks after the pets, ensuring they have the food and medications you've supplied; you can be with your pet jnt.im/424 during the hours the kennels are open each day. The price is steep, but not prohibitive, and you might consider taking the QM2 to Southampton, then returning by air.

LOCAL CRUISES

As with bus travel, regional options — in this case, local and day cruises — are more likely to be pet-friendly. If a web site doesn't mention a pet policy, pick up the phone. With luck, you'll find an option like these:

☞ Maine's Casco Bay Line jnt.im/426, a ferry company which offers day cruises around the islands off Portland (your leashed dog is welcome), and Acadian Nature Cruises jnt.im/422, offering pet-friendly sightseeing and nature cruises from Bar Harbor

☞ Florida's Calusa Queen jnt.im/423, welcoming small and mid-sized dogs

A less glamorous, but still appealing, option is to travel as a passenger on a cargo ship. Most of the global shipping lines offer passenger cabins; nearly all, however, forbid passengers to bring pets with them. You may find the rare exception, but prepare for disappointment.

on six of its seven eco-tours around Charlotte Harbor

☞ The Shell Key Shuttle jnt.im/449, taking owners and dogs on a sunset cruise around the waterways and barrier islands off St. Pete Beach

☞ Mercury Cruise's seasonal (summer only) Canine Chicago Cruise jnt.im/418 of Chicago's waterways ("Don't worry, we have one restroom for humans and one lined with newspapers for your pet.")

☞ It's a bit of a stretch to call it a cruise, but the pet-friendly Charleston Water Taxi jnt.im/419 (leashed dogs welcome) will give you a great view of the harbor, including Fort Sumter.

☞ Cruise the harbors of Annapolis or Baltimore, or poke around the Chesapeake Bay, with Cruises on the Bay by Watermark jnt.im/417 — all of the cruises are leashed-dog-friendly.

☞ The Staten Island Ferry jnt.im/420 will bring you and your muzzled pet as close as you can get, together, to the Statue of Liberty

☞ San Francisco's Blue & Gold Fleet jnt.im/415 will take you and your leashed dog on a couple of don't-miss harbor trips (Pier 41 to either Tiburon or Sausalito, and the Bay Cruise Adventure)

☞ Another don't-miss trip is the ferry ride from Sydney jnt.im/416's Circular Quay ferry terminal to Manly Terminal and back; your pet will have to be small enough, however, to tuck into a carrier during the trip

☞ The little "pickle boats" plying the harbor in Victoria, B.C. welcome pets on board

You could, in fact, take the Alaska State Ferry jnt.im/414 from Bellingham, WA to Skagway, by way of the Inside Passage, but your pet would have to be crated or contained on the car deck (you are permitted to visit her "several" times a day).

TRAVELING BY FERRY

Setting aside for the moment their sightseeing potential, ferries are a practical way to get from one place to another, and more often than not, pets are allowed on board. Aside from the ferries listed in the "Local Cruises" section above, leashed dogs and small pets in carriers are permitted on:

☞ Washington State ferries and Vancouver's BC Ferries jnt.im/421

☞ Long Island jnt.im/410's Bridgeport & Port Jefferson ferry and the Orient Point ferry

☞ The Island Queen jnt.im/411 ferry from Falmouth to Martha's Vineyard

☞ Most Block Island jnt.im/409 ferries

☞ All three ferry companies serving Mackinac Islan jnt.im/412 d

☞ The boats serving Maine's Monhegan Island jnt.im/408 jnt.im/389

Abroad, travel with your dog to Brittany's Iles de Morbihan jnt.im/413 (including Belle-Ile-en-Mer) from Quiberon, or to Ireland's gorgeous Aran Islands jnt.im/406, in Galway Bay.

Carry a soft muzzle with you, in case it turns out to be needed (*e.g.,* on the ferries to Staten Island or California's Catalina Island jnt.im/164). Your Chihuahua may look a little goofy in a tiny muzzle, but she may prefer it to spending the crossing in a carrier.

Take a ferry to Corsica jnt.im/405 or to Gotland jnt.im/407, or sail on the Grandi Navi Veloci jnt.im/404 ferries from Genoa to Tangiers, and then back to Barcelona (one option of many!).

Traveling by ferry to the U.K. has a certain amount of inherent appeal, but it's also one of the limited number of ways that pets are allowed to enter the U.K. The DEFRA pet travel page jnt.im/401 maintains a list of approved ferry lines jnt.im/402; take a look and see which leave from the location that works best with your travel plans. Seat 61 jnt.im/400 is an excellent resource for more details about pet travel by ferry to and from the U.K.

There are many variations in the companies' requirements, so read the fine print and call for details. If you learn that you will need to stay on an open deck with your dog, bring warm jackets for both of you, even in mild weather. You are traveling over a body of water, so the leash and carrier requirements make sense, and should be observed. Keep an eye on your pet and make sure she's comfortable and sufficiently hydrated. Give her a good walk before boarding, to avoid accidents and encourage snoozing.

CRUISING WITH YOUR PET

You may already have a sailboat of your own; if not, you might be thinking about renting one — or perhaps renting a houseboat, or a canal boat. Here's a list of dog-friendly options to consider as you rummage in your closet for your beloved topsiders:

☞ How about renting a houseboat on Nevada's Lake Mead, about 45 minutes' drive from Las Vegas? Forever

In some instances, you'll find that you and your pet can travel by ferry to a destination, but in different parts of the boat. For example, a crossing from Portsmouth to Caen on Brittany Ferries takes either about four hours or 6-7 hours; depending on the ship, your pet will either jnt.im/162 stay in your car on the vehicle deck, travel in a rented kennel, or share a dog-friendly cabin with you. Traveling to the Orkney Islands (about 5-6 hours) and then on to the Shetland Islands (7-8 hours), your pet will travel in a rented kennel jnt.im/163, and you can visit him, and exercise him on the outer decks, on request and at the crew's convenience. On the other side of the globe, when you cross Cook Strait jnt.im/160 by ferry (a 3-hour trip), your pet will travel on the vehicle deck, either in a rented kennel or in your car, and if you take the ferry to Tasmania jnt.im/161 (a 9-hour trip), your pet will travel in a rented kennel.

If you know your pet will be traveling in a rented kennel, stock up ahead of time on cleaning wipes, and wipe down the kennel's interior. Leave your dog with comfortable padding and a stable water bowl. Think about whether the tags on his collar might get caught in the grating of his kennel; if possible, leave him in a collar with your cell phone number woven into it, so tags aren't necessary. Because he'll be in close proximity to other pets, congratulate yourself on keeping his bordetella (kennel cough) vaccine current. And if you anticipate a rough crossing, dose your pet with the anti-seasickness remedy you and your vet decided on.

Resorts jnt.im/403 rents houseboats of different sizes at the Callville marina; pets are allowed on any boat, for a non-refundable fee of $100 per pet.

☞ Rent a houseboat on Lake Shasta jnt.im/396, in northern California, and you'll only pay extra if your pet damages the boat, or if the boat requires extra cleaning.

☞ Travel New York's Erie Canal on the two boats Mid-Lakes Navigation jnt.im/395 offers to small dog owners

☞ Many European countries have extensive canal systems, and you'll find plenty of pet-friendly options jnt.im/397

☞ Explore the Norfolk Broads, a protected area of navigable waterways in eastern England, by boat with your pet — no locks to negotiate, and the area is an angler's and bird watcher's dream — at Richardson's Boating Holidays jnt.im/394, pets are expected on board (you need to check the "no pets" box if you want a boat that *doesn't* welcome pets)

☞ Black Prince jnt.im/398 offers pet-friendly narrowboat and barge rentals jnt.im/393 from eight bases scattered across England, Wales, and Scotland

However you choose to cruise, you will want to look after your pet's safety and comfort:

➤ Buy your pet a life jacket (buoyant foam jackets jnt.im/392 are most common, but there is one automatic inflatable PFD jnt.im/399 for pets) and have him wear it. Even dogs who swim — and not all do — cannot swim for long, especially in cold water or in a current. The best pet life jackets have a handle on the top so you can grab them out of the water from above. Attach a

Finding a bareboat yacht charter company that allows dogs or cats on board is nearly impossible, probably because the owners fear damage to decks from your pet's claws. One possible lead is Vancouver, B.C.'s Blue Pacific Yacht Charters jnt.im/158. There are a few charter companies that welcome your pet on captained day cruises, including Enchanted Charters jnt.im/159 (waterway and offshore cruises near South Carolina's Myrtle Beach) and Dog Gone Sailing Charters jnt.im/157 (Moondance II, a 30' cutter, will carry you and several guests on excursions from Provincetown).

water-activated flashing light jnt.im/389 to it, for nighttime emergencies.

➤ If you are outfitting your own boat, add safety netting along the lifelines. A tether jnt.im/390 can be very helpful, but ensure that your pet won't choke himself with it by attaching it to his harness (not his collar) and keeping it short. Assess your tethered pet's surroundings for things or features a tether could snag on, and never leave your pet on a tether when you're absent from the boat. When you leave your pet behind, close him in the cabin (be sure it's ventilated and cool!) or crate him instead.

➤ Give your pet the skills he needs to help rescue himself by training him (in short sessions on pleasant days, when the boat is docked) to be comfortable in his life jacket, to swim in it briefly, and to swim in it to a spot by the boat where he can be reached with a hand or, if he's very small, a fishing net.

➤ Take time to get your pet accustomed to the sounds and movements of a boat. In easy steps, bring your pet on board,

> Cats can do a great deal to rescue themselves if they are taught to find a piece of carpeting or a towel attached to your boat near the waterline and left trailing in the water. (In fact, you may decide that your cat's life jacket is preventing him from swimming well — it's not always easy to fit a cat — and that he's better served by good training on the trailing towel.)

then turn on the motor, then take a very short cruise, then increase the length of your outings. Spread the process out as much as you can, and at each step, be generous with encouragement, praise and treats. Make sure, too, that your pet is on a leash, in case any of the steps surprises him into sudden movement.

Like you, your pup may get seasick, and should be protected from the weather. Here are some tips to keep him comfortable while you're underway:

➤ Talk to your vet before you leave and get a prescription for the motion sickness medication best suited for your pet. If your pup is prone to seasickness at the beginning of a trip (or if this is uncharted territory for him), hold off feeding him for several hours before you start moving. Secure your pet (in a crate or on a tether) towards the center of the boat, where the motion is less

> Ideally, your cat's litter box will be in the central, least active part of the boat, and won't shift around while you're underway. To reduce litter scatter, consider a covered top-entry option like the Clevercat jnt.im/126 litter box. If storing and disposing of litter isn't appealing, consider a litter-free alternative jnt.im/127, or teach your cat to use the head jnt.im/125.

extreme. The good news is that, as with humans, your pet will eventually come to terms with a boat's normal motion.

➤ Protect your pet from too much sun, and from overheating. Options for canine cooling jackets include the Chillybuddy jacket jnt.im/388 and the Ruffwear Swamp Cooler jnt.im/391.

➤ If you're wearing sunglasses, chances are your dog should be too jnt.im/386.

➤ Check the deck every so often with your hand — if it's hot to the touch, it'll be hot to the paw. Bring a pair of booties in case your pup needs them (and make sure they're non-skid, so your pup can keep his footing on smooth and often wet decking).

➤ Make sure your pet has access to water — a Buddy Bowl jnt.im/387 will prevent spills even in rough seas.

And, finally, keep "poop deck" a joke by figuring out how your pet can relieve himself on board. In a moored boat, you can keep an eye out for your dog's gotta-go signal, and ferry him ashore. An attractive shipboard option jnt.im/384 is the Pup Head, which comes in three sizes, simulates grass, and lasts up to five years. Keep it clean jnt.im/385 by rinsing the turf with a weekly swish through seawater (wash the base with soap and water), and a monthly soak in an enzymatic solution. It will likely take a little time to train your dog to use it, particularly if he first learned to go outdoors, but it can be done.

If you need to be convinced that cruising with your dog is a good idea, do a quick search on Flickr for "dog sailing" and see the joy for yourself. Having a dog on board adds a kind of companionship you'll love, and he's likely to improve your sense of security (even if he's a pushover, he'll at least alert you to the arrival of unwanted visitors). You'll need to take some basic steps to ensure that he's safe and comfortable, but you'll never regret adding your pup to your crew list.

7

Tail wind: Flying with your pet

U nless you and Fifi are traveling in your own private jet, you have three options: A small pet can travel in-cabin with you on many airlines (though not all, and not to all destinations); a larger dog can travel as checked baggage (on your plane); and a pet can travel as cargo (on a different plane than yours).

BEFORE YOU TRAVEL

You'll need to prepare for flying with your pet by purchasing an in-cabin carrier, or a crate (if your pet is traveling as checked baggage or cargo), far enough in advance of your flight that your pet has a chance to get comfortable with it. You will also need to make a reservation for your pet on your plane (if you're traveling together), or on her plane (if she's traveling as cargo).

MAKING A PLANE RESER-VATION FOR YOUR PET

I'm starting with this to-do item, even though it might happen in time *after* you buy your pet's carrier/crate (you really do want to give a pet new to travel a lot of time to learn to love her carrier), because it's relatively straightforward.

Pets traveling in the plane's belly
Nearly every major U.S. airline requires that you make a reservation for your checked pet jnt.im/380. The exception

is American Airlines jnt.im/381, which makes it clear that your checked pet will be "accepted on a first-come basis." If you are traveling with a checked pet on American, show up earlier than you would otherwise, to be sure your pet makes it on the plane with you. When you make your pet's reservation on other airlines, confirm with the ticketing agent that your pet has a guaranteed spot on board.

As you know from news reports, traveling in the baggage compartment has its risks. PetFlight.com jnt.im/378 posts monthly and annual reports of "pet related airline incidents," including deaths, injuries and losses. Details suggest that many of the incidents (this article jnt.im/379 focused on a 2011 DOT report) could be avoided if the airlines followed their own rules about transporting pets with medical conditions, and transporting pets during the summer. Help prevent an incident by honestly assessing your pet's condition, refraining from tranquilizing her, and opting to fly when the weather is temperate. Try to fly mid-week, and not during a holiday rush, when handlers may be distracted. Review the available pet incident reports, read an airline's pet handling policies closely (and follow up with questions), and decide which airline seems to be handling pets best.

In-cabin pets
Since most U.S. airlines also have a limited number of available spots for in-cabin pets, you will also need to make a reservation when you and your pet are traveling in the passenger cabin. Your pet will travel under the seat in front of you (even if you buy a second ticket, her carrier cannot rest on the seat). Do what research you

Please note that you will not be allowed to travel in bulkhead or exit row seats with your in-cabin pet. When possible, and if your budget allows, get a seat with extra legroom. The space will let you bend over and administer pats, treats and ice cubes to your pet without getting too intimate with your neighbor.

can, therefore, to select a seat where the space underneath is not limited by boxes for the plane's electronic system or by metal rails. Dog Jaunt is gathering under-seat measurements `jnt.im/382`, and is a good place to start.

Be sure to read the airlines' pet policies carefully. Your airline may not allow an in-cabin pet to travel to certain destinations. For example, until recently, the only way to take your pet in-cabin to Hawaii was on Korean Air, traveling through Incheon. In August 2011, Alaska Airlines quietly modified its pet policy `jnt.im/377` to "accept cats and dogs only for travel to and from Hawaii," including in cabin. The problem may be with the country, not the airline: Pets cannot arrive in-cabin on flights to the U.K., Ireland `jnt.im/376`, Australia `jnt.im/375`, or New Zealand `jnt.im/383` (there also appears to be no way to bring your

Two U.S. airlines — Southwest and U.S. Airways — will not guarantee `jnt.im/156` your in-cabin pet a place on board, even if you call ahead of time and add her to your ticket. While it would be unusual for there to be so many in-cabin pets on one flight that the quota gets filled, I suggest showing up a little earlier than you normally would when flying with a pet on those airlines during the holidays, or other peak travel times.

pet in-cabin to South Africa `jnt.im/372`, Kenya `jnt.im/373`, or Hong Kong `jnt.im/371` – destinations I chose randomly to see what the rules would say).

One U.S. airline (Virgin America) allows you to make your pet's reservation on-line, at the same time yours is made. Four airlines (Allegiant, Frontier, JetBlue and Sun Country) either don't have a phone booking fee, or waive your phone booking fee, so you can call and make your own reservation, adding your dog at the same time, without incurring a financial penalty (be sure to remind your reservations agent to waive your fee). The remaining airlines don't waive the phone booking fee: Your only alternative to paying it is to call ahead, determine if there's room for an in-cabin pet on your flight, make your own reservation on-line, then call back immediately to add your pet to your reservation.

International airlines are cagier about how many in-cabin pets they allow per flight, and whether they will waive a phone booking fee if you are traveling with a pet. Call first and ask whether you can make your reservations together without incurring a fee. If not, ask whether there is space on your flight for your in-cabin pet, then make your own reservation on-line and call back to add your pet. Confirm with the reservations agent that

Whenever you have a conversation with an airline agent about your pet's travel arrangements, take their name and make a note of the date and gist of the conversation. Bring your notes with you to the airport, in case you have to prove that the arrangements have, indeed, been made.

your pet now has a guaranteed place in the passenger cabin on your flight.

IN-CABIN PET CARRIERS

If you have a small pet (say, under 10 pounds), you have several excellent options. Well-designed and well-made choices include Sturdi Products' small SturdiBag jnt.im/374 carrier, Sleepypod's Air jnt.im/369 carrier, and the regular Kobi jnt.im/370 carrier. The Kobi bag can expand in length, while the Air bag can be temporarily shortened. The SturdiBag carrier changes shape in a different way: Its top and sides are so flexible that it can fit in oddly-shaped spaces.

If you, like me, have a larger small pet (between 10 and 20 pounds) and want to carry her in cabin, I recommend the large SturdiBag jnt.im/368 carrier. At 18″ × 12″ × 12″, it may be larger than many U.S. and international airlines' stated maximums, but the flexibility of its top and sides let it work in most under seat spaces. It also provides excellent patting and visual access to your pet from above, which is important for a pet who will spend hours at your feet. Another good choice for a larger small dog is the large Kobi jnt.im/367 carrier; it's heavier than the SturdiBag, but especially on long-haul flights, your pet will really appreciate the optional extra three inches of length you can add by unzipping a gusset. I recommend buying the SturdiBag in black, or the Kobi in charcoal, to minimize your carrier's perceived size. Please note that the extra-large SturdiBag is substantially larger, and may be questioned by ticketing and gate agents.

Your in-cabin carrier should be as tall as your pet's shoulder height. Airlines require, and may enforce their

Your bird will travel best in a small, hard-sided PetMate Cabin Kennel jnt.im/153 or in Celltei's marvelous In-Cabin Airline Travel Bird Carrier jnt.im/154.

requirement, that pets be able to turn around easily in their in-cabin carrier. The remaining requirements are, typically, a moisture-proof bottom, adequate ventilation, and a secure closure. Be mindful of an airline's stated upper weight limit for in-cabin pets; every so often you'll encounter a ticketing agent who weighs your pet and her carrier.

If the padded bottom of your pet's carrier seems too firm, add a padded mat (keep it slim if your pet's headroom is an issue) or other soft bedding. An unlaundered t-shirt of yours is a good choice. If you are concerned that your pet may have an accident en route, line the carrier with a DryFur pad jnt.im/364 (the medium size works for a large SturdiBag carrier). If your pet has a favorite toy, bring it, unless it occupies too much carrier real estate.

CRATES FOR CHECKED OR CARGO PETS

The PetMate Sky Kennel jnt.im/365 is an excellent crate choice, because it is made of rigid plastic, and has ventilation panels on four sides (required for international travel), "spacer bars" around its perimeter

If you are concerned that your cat's claws will make short work of ventilation panels, consider the Sherpa Cat Tote jnt.im/155, which has wire mesh ventilation. Alternatively, for a small additional cost, Sturdi Products will send you a carrier with extra-sturdy nylon mesh paneling (though their normal mesh paneling is good quality).

(to keep carriers from being packed too tightly together, and for easy lifting and handling), and a sturdy closure for its metal door. It is constructed with nuts and bolts (not a twist lock or snap lock). Crates used for checked animals must not be made of wire, and if they have wheels, the wheels must be removed.

Choose a size that allows your pet to stand up (head erect jnt.im/366, not bent down), turn around and lie down comfortably. If your dog is too large for the "Series 700" crate, you can have a crate constructed for you, following the guidelines in the USDA and IATA documents.

PREPARING YOUR PET'S CRATE FOR TRAVEL

You've bought your pet's crate, it's the right size, and she's comfortable in it. Is your work done? Nope. It's time to pimp your crate:

➤ Although the PetMate kennels come with nuts and bolts, the standard bolt has a plastic wing nut. For added security (and to meet the require-

The USDA and International Air Transport Association (IATA) have both published regulations for shipping live animals. The USDA's rules jnt.im/151 (see Section 3.13 and following) and the IATA's Container Requirement jnt.im/152 describe acceptable construction and labeling for cargo-area airplane crates. The largest size allowed on U.S. and international flights varies by airline, but for checked pets it's typically the "Series 500" size (also known as the extra-large PetMate Sky Kennel; the Giant, or "Series 700" size, is sometimes allowed, and please note that there is no "Series 600" size).

A pet relocation service like PetRelocation.com jnt.im/150 can help you with all aspects of your pet's transportation, including assembling the documents your pet needs, reserving her a space on the plane, picking her up at your home, bringing her to the airport, clearing her through customs on arrival and delivering her to you at your destination. They would be a good resource for getting a custom crate constructed.

ments of airlines like Delta jnt.im/361, which require metal nuts and bolts), replace the provided hardware with all-metal hardware jnt.im/362.

➤ American requires that the door on checked crates be secured not only by the carrier's own spring latch but also by "releasable cable ties attached to all four corners jnt.im/360." Even if your airline doesn't require it, it's a good idea, since you want to ensure that your pet doesn't escape. Make sure the cable ties are "releasable jnt.im/363," not "locking", and leave finger room when you cinch them closed, so they're secure but you (or someone else, in a delay or layover situation) can access the release mechanism. Check to see that the ends won't rotate into your pet's compartment, where she might be tempted to chew on them.

➤ The carrier must be marked with a "Live Animals" sticker (letters at least an inch high) and arrowed "This Way Up" stickers on all four sides, if possible. Your airline may have the stickers, but who needs to be labeling a crate last minute? Instead, buy a

Before the day of travel, trim your pet's nails, to reduce the chance they'll be damaged if she claws her crate.

set of stickers ahead of time (the Deluxe set `jnt.im/358` is better because it has three "This Way Up" labels).

➤ The Deluxe set comes with a "shipper's declaration form" and a "kennel tag," which is a reminder that you need to attach to your pet's crate a written declaration `jnt.im/359` (see Section 3.13 of the USDA's rules `jnt.im/357`) that you have offered her food and water within four hours of handing her over to the airline.

➤ The crate should also be labeled with your name, address and telephone number, your flight information, and contact information for you at your destination address.

➤ If your pet is embarking on a long flight and will need one or more meals en route, put portions of her kibble in a resealable zippered storage bag (double-bag it for added protection) and tape it to her crate. Write down how much she should receive, and when, and attach the instructions to her crate (the shipper's declaration form you've purchased has room on it; alternatively, create a separate label with food instructions and tape that to her crate).

➤ Consider taping a leash to the top of the crate (a plastic bag will keep it corralled): Your pet won't ordinarily

Ideally, your pet would also have a tag on her collar, with contact information for you (including your destination information). On the other hand, a dangling tag can be a choking hazard, especially in an unattended crate. A better solution is a flat collar with your cell phone information woven into it `jnt.im/149` or a collar that incorporates a panel with a QR code `jnt.im/148` — still flat, but the information can be updated or supplemented at will.

Verify that the tape you're using will not peel off your crate's plastic surface; if it's not sticking well, rough up the crate's surface with sandpaper and try again.

leave her enclosure, but if there's an emergency or a serious delay and she needs to, you don't want her handler to improvise (or do without).

➤ To improve the chances that the handlers encountering your pet's crate will treat it and your pet with extra care, tape a picture of your pet to the crate, and put her name on it too.

➤ Make her crate stand out, and be easily visible, by putting lengths of fluorescent duct tape `jnt.im/354` on the bits of the crate that aren't now covered by labels and food packets.

➤ As with an in-cabin carrier, the base of the crate must be moisture-proof. Line it with absorbent material — Delta suggests shredded paper or towels (hay, straw and wood shavings are not allowed by American, and may not be by others). A better choice is DryFur's "breathable" super-absorbent crate pad `jnt.im/355`, which comes in a large sheet, wicks moisture away from your pet, and can be taped down to the crate's floor, or around a crate pad, so it won't shift in transit. Put some more soft bedding on top, including a tee-shirt you've worn (she'll appreciate the reminder of you).

➤ There must be at least one water dish in your pet's crate (two gives your pet a back up if the first runs low). It needs to be accessible from the outside; in practice, this means that the dish clips on to your crate's door, and a handler can refill it by poking a

Your crate will likely come with a small plastic dish, but consider replacing it with, or adding, transparent (so handlers can see how much water your pet has), spill-resistant dishes jnt.im/102 in the substantial L/XL size. It's a good idea to freeze the water in your pet's two water dishes; it'll melt as the day goes along, and cut down on spillage.

water bottle or the nozzle of a watering can through the door's grating.

ON THE DAY OF TRAVEL

No matter what size your pet is, or where she's traveling in the plane, provide her with plenty of exercise before you leave for the airport. A tired pet is a good traveler. You will need to sign a statement that you have offered your checked pet food and water within four hours of handing her over to the airline; an in-cabin pet, similarly, should have her food picked up several hours before departure (she won't starve, with all the treats you'll be giving her en route) and her water should be picked up about two hours before departure.

AT THE AIRPORT AND ON THE PLANE WITH AN IN-CABIN PET

Your pet must be fully enclosed in her carrier when you enter the airport, and must remain in her carrier at the airport and on the plane. You will see pictures of stars walking their pets through LAX, and you may encounter a non-celebrity pet out of her carrier, but in nearly every airport the rules require pets to be contained. If your carrier has large ventilation panels, she will be able to see what's going on

— and there is no rule against reaching your hand in to her carrier to pat her.

Because you are traveling with a pet, you'll need to check in at the front desk. If you haven't already paid for your pet, you'll be asked for payment now. If paperwork is required for your flight, you'll be asked for it now. You may get a tag for your pet's carrier, and your pet may be weighed (in her carrier), though that's rare.

If you are traveling with a pet who pushes an airline's maximums, improve your chances that the ticketing agent will overlook her size by keeping your carrier at your feet while you're checking in. When it comes time to pay the pet fee, mention, casually, that you're traveling with an in-cabin pet. If you're asked to present the carrier for tagging, lift it as if it weighed nothing. Do not grunt. Do not volunteer that you are concerned about getting her on board. Convey the impression that you do this all the time, and that you are cheerfully confident about your travel day together. Nod happily when the airline agent asks you if you're aware of the rules relating to in-cabin dogs, and mention what a good little traveler your girl is.

If push comes to shove, demonstrate how well your carrier flexes to fit tough spots (this will work best with the delightfully flexible SturdiBag), and show the agent pictures of your carrier on previous flights (if you don't have a collection of your own started, use the ones I'm collecting on Dog Jaunt jnt.im/356).

GOING THROUGH SECURITY

As you approach the moving belt that carries your belongings through the x-ray machine, fish out a really great dog treat and hold it in your hand while you

> Keep the tag from your last flight on your pet's carrier, even if you're usually the type to tidy up your luggage between flights. Seeing it, even if it's from another airline, is likely to help persuade a ticketing agent that your pet's carrier is workable.

remove your shoes and fill bins with your outerwear and toiletries and laptop. Push those bins onto the moving belt. Then put your pet's carrier on a solid surface in front of the moving belt (there's usually some kind of table or platform) and unzip it. Extract your pet, toss the treat into the depths of the carrier while she's watching, and zip the carrier loosely closed. Holding your pet in your arms, push the carrier onto the belt, followed by your "personal item" or your companion's carry-on (the weight will keep your pet's empty carrier from getting stuck in the x-ray machine).

Walk through the detector when you're gestured through (a traveler with a pet in arms will typically be sent through a traditional metal detector, not the new whole-body imaging scanners). Your pet's collar will not usually set off the alarm. If it does, back up, take it off and put it in a bowl to be sent through separately. Walk through again.

In U.S. airports, you will have your hands swabbed by a security official before you're reunited with your pet's carrier. Wait to be called over to the side, and when directed hold out one hand and then the other (shifting your pet around in your arms as you do so). If your pet is likely to resent the TSA official's presence, ask if you can put her back in her carrier before having your hands swabbed.

Do not put your pet back in her carrier on the rollers that lead away from the machine, since they can pinch body parts and they're alarmingly noisy — instead, push her carrier down to the solid end of the ramp, or bring her carrier over to another solid surface, before putting her back in. Nervousness about her surroundings, and the allure of the treat you tossed in, will usually make re-entry easy.

ONBOARD WITH AN IN-CABIN PET

When you board the plane, stow your personal item in the overhead bin and fit your pet's carrier under the seat in front of you. Depending on the configuration of the under-seat space, your carrier will either be oriented left-to-right or front-to-back. It will help your pet if she can see you through one of her carrier's ventilation panels, and if you can reach in to pat her or drop her treats. You may be able to pull your pet's carrier out under your knees during the flight, and you may even be allowed to put her carrier on your lap, but you may not allow any part of her to poke of out her carrier.

Airlines leave it in the hands of allergic passengers to inquire whether their flight has pets on board. Help your neighbors by letting them know you're traveling with a pet, so they can request to be re-seated before the boarding process is over. Win your seatmates' hearts by showing them a picture of your pet — knowing what she looks like, and the chatting that accompanies picture sharing, may buy you some tolerance if your pet whines later, or if your neighbor needs to step over her carrier to reach the aisle.

During the flight, distract a bored pet with a toy or a chew. Whenever the beverage service comes around, give your dog a couple of ice cubes (your cat may drink from a shallow dish — bring a jar lid with you, just in case — but it's unlikely). Your goal is to keep your pet hydrated, without making her desperate for the bathroom.

How about food? You organized her intake so she's boarding with an empty stomach (and gut), but a very long travel day without food, or with just treats, may be too hard on her system. I've recently begun bringing a small resealable zippered storage bag of Chloe's kibble with me – just a meal's worth – and dispensing it to her one or two pieces at a time over the course of the day. My theory is that it provides her with better nutrition than the liver or cheese puffs I use as treats, and the slow dosage improves the chances that she'll only need to poop after we land.

Keep a foot, preferably shoe-free, next to your pet's carrier during flight so that you know what kind of temperatures she's experiencing down there. Often it's quite chilly, especially in a window seat, and you'll want to poke your sweater or jacket alongside her to cut off the draft. An even nastier problem is when it's hot. Direct your air vent towards her carrier, and ask if you can borrow your neighbor's, too, if it's not in use. Bring along a small, battery-powered fan jnt.im/353, and make sure all of your pet's carrier's privacy panels are rolled up and out of the way. If it gets really warm, ask a flight attendant to turn down the cabin temperature (given how hard they're working, they're likely to be feeling the heat too).

On a very long flight, you can take your pet, in her carrier, to the restroom (choose a time when most people are sleeping or watching a movie), let her stretch, and have her run through her

Cats will likely decline to use the bathroom on a plane trip, but on a very long flight even the most determined cat may change her mind. Slip a folding litter box and a resealable zippered storage bag of litter in your small personal item or your companion's carry-on, and give it a try.

tricks and skills. If your pet is trained to use a pee-pad, she can take the pause that refreshes. Otherwise, she'll need to wait until you land and can find her a pet relief area or a patch of grass.

AT THE AIRPORT AND ON THE PLANE WITH A CHECKED PET

To be perfectly correct, find a cart when you arrive at the airport, load your pet in her travel crate onto it, and roll it with your luggage up to the ticketing counter. If a cart is not available, the ticketing agents will turn a blind eye to your Golden Retriever walking up to the counter with you (you have, after all, removed any wheels your crate had). The ticketing agent will collect payment for your pet, if you haven't prepaid, and will review your paperwork.

Your pet will join you briefly while her crate is sent through the x-ray machine. Then she goes back in (sweeten the deal with some treats), and you'll secure the crate door with releasable cable ties, if you've brought them.

Review with the ticketing agent the materials and information you've taped to the crate. Sign the shipper's declaration (stating that your pet has been offered food and water within the past four hours). Confirm that your pet will be traveling in a ventilated and temperature-controlled area of the plane.

Ask where you need to go, and what you need to do, to meet your pet at your destination. If you will be making a connection, find out how to collect your pet and check her onto the second flight (the airline may offer to handle the transfer for you, but it's a valuable opportunity for you to see your pet, assess her condition, and give her some love).

From this point forward, tell every airline agent you meet about your checked pet. Let the gate agent know about her when you reach the boarding area, and tell the flight crew when you arrive on the plane. Ask to speak to the captain: Reconfirm that your pet will be traveling in a ventilated and temperature-controlled compartment, and ask to be notified when your pet has been put on the plane. Inquire about the outside temperature, and the temperature in the baggage compartment.

Keep an eye on the time. If there is a delay, ask again about the temperature in your pet's compartment. If it is a hot day and your flight is held at the gate or on the tarmac for a significant period of time, insist that your pet be brought out for observation, water, and relief from the heat. Do your best to be there when your pet is brought out, since you know how she behaves and how she appeared when she left your care. If the delay is substantial, ask to claim your pet, and take her for a walk. Be polite, but be firm. In this situation, you are your pet's advocate.

When you land, thank the crew for their help and immediately locate your pet and give her water. Depending on the airport, you may be able to let her relieve herself before you clear customs. Collect your luggage and exit, either directly or through customs.

It's a clever (and kind) idea to give the flight crew a box of chocolates while you're talking with them, and thank them in advance for their kindness and support. If you make a gift tag from a particularly adorable picture of your pet, they'll have her face in mind when you approach them with your concerns.

PET RELIEF AREAS

All U.S. airports are now required to have a "pet relief area jnt.im/352," a designated spot where service animals (and pets) can relieve themselves. Some have fencing, and a bench, and a water fountain and some have just a supply of poop bags and a trashcan. Nearly all are on the land side of security, meaning that if you want to visit them with your pet during a layover, you will need to leave the secured area, find the pet relief area, and then return through security. That process typically takes about an hour (a long security line, of course, will slow you down), so schedule your flights and layovers accordingly.

For example, if you're arriving at Paris's Charles de Gaulle airport on an airplane that arrives at Terminal 1 (the round one, with the people-moving tubes), your immediate choices are limited to a thin strip of planting next to the sidewalk, and a daunting slope of greenery just across the roadways that circle the terminal. Looking at an airport map, though, you'll see there's a Hotel Ibis at CDG, which you can reach via the inter-terminal tram (the CDGVAL) — and Google Maps reveals that it is landscaped with small lawns. Be sure to bring, and use, your own poop bag. Also, please note that the Hotel Ibis chain is pet-friendly, so this might be a good place for you and your pet to stay if you have an early departure from Roissy.

A handful of airports (including Washington D.C.'s Dulles International Airport and the airports in Dallas, Minneapolis-St. Paul, Pittsburgh, Salt Lake City, Seattle, and San Diego) have pet relief areas on the *air* side of security, which makes a pet owner's life much easier.

Some Canadian airports also have pet relief areas, but outside North America you'll need to rely on your own research to find a suitable spot for Spot. Start by visiting the airport's web site and familiarizing yourself with the airport's map. Then look at the airport on Google Maps, using the satellite view to find likely patches of grass. Often, big airports will have airport hotels, which typically have a bit of lawn nearby.

If your pet is trained to use a pee-pad, one alternative is to use a bathroom stall. Wait until there is no demand for the stall, be generous with your pee pads even if you are confident your pet has pinpoint aim, and clean up thoroughly.

Flying with a pet is what I get the most questions about on my blog, Dog Jaunt, so I know it's something that concerns you. I'm here to tell you that despite all these details, it's a pretty straightforward process. Your first trip may have its awkward moments as you get used to adding a couple of new steps to your usual routine, but it's very doable. And it just gets easier — soon you'll be sending me travel tips (I welcome them, by the way)!

8

On foot and by bike

Snap a leash on your dog, put your bird on your shoulder (or your ferret in his backpack) — you've arrived at your destination and it's time to step outside. This section focuses first on walking with your pet, whether it's in town or on the trail. Feeling sociable? Other pets are out there with their owners — meet them at dog parks, or meet-ups. Alternatively, put your foot down, and then put the other one down: You're biking, and with a bit of preparation, your pet can keep you company.

WALKING AND HIKING WITH YOUR PET

If there's one thing you already know how to do, it's walk your dog. I understand that – these are just a few tips to help make walking him in a new environment safer and more comfortable for you both.

LEASH CHOICES

Leash choices are a big part of being a responsible pet owner. More often than not, there are good reasons behind a location's posted leash rules. Also, even if your dog behaves well off-leash, and has a completely dependable recall, another person's leashed dog may react poorly to your roaming dog.

If you're in a location where a leash is not required, think about whether a leash might protect your dog from hazards like wildlife (always use a leash in bear country, or where you're likely to encounter snakes), unexpected terrain changes, currents (if you're near a body of water), or simply getting too far away from you to find his way back.

Another reason to keep your dog on a leash in the woods? A roaming dog may brush against poison ivy or poison oak, which won't bother him — but will bother you when you touch the sap he's carried back on his fur.

A collection of leashes will let you choose the one that's most appropriate for each outing. A retractable leash (e.g., Flexi) is an excellent choice for a dog with uncertain swimming abilities walking with you on an empty beach, but it's a bad choice in a forest, or for in-city walking, unless it's locked at its shortest length — and in that case, why bother with its clunky handle? Select instead a 6-foot long leash with a looped handle you can pass your hand through for added security. If you're a runner, consider a leash that clips around your waist and leaves your hands free.

There's no poison ivy in Europe, you're thinking, but Europe has hiking hazards of its own, including, for example, the Pine Processionary Caterpillar, which can cause serious (and sometimes fatal) harm to dogs and their owners if the tiny barbed hairs that cover them are touched or ingested. Look out for them in pine trees and forests in Spain and elsewhere in Southern Europe. Their name tells you their distinguishing feature: When they're on the move, starting in about January and continuing through April, the caterpillars travel in a long chain, or procession.

URBAN WALKS

Walking your dog, an everyday job at home, is a reason in itself to go somewhere else. With a dog, you'll walk through neighborhoods at a pace that allows you to see details you'd miss in a vehicle. If your dog is attractive and approachable, you will meet locals at every turn, and at their warmest, goofiest best. You'll look, and feel, like a local yourself, which may be misleading, but is certainly a pleasure.

When you set off for the day, pack a dog water bottle and poop bags in your day bag. Research the pet rules for the parks you plan to visit, and for the transit systems you might use. If you anticipate bringing your small dog on public transit, or walking his paws off, bring a collapsible tote with you (recall that most public transit systems that allow pets require them to be in a closed carrier).

Taxis are not required to take a fare with a pet, but may if your pet looks well mannered and you ask nicely. A small pet in a closed carrier is nearly always a shoo-in.

A surprising number of stores will let you enter with your pet dog. In some communities, a sign on the door signals that dogs are welcome; more commonly, you'll need to ask. Wait in the doorway with your dog and ask if you may come in; show the right attitude by offering to carry your small dog. If you're allowed inside, make sure that your dog stays by you and away from the merchandise.

TRAIL WALKING

Let's start with the bad news: Pet dogs are not particularly welcome in U.S. National Parks. If you're hoping to experience Yellowstone National Park with your dog, you'll be disappointed: Pets are "prohibited in the backcountry and on trails and boardwalks," and allowed, leashed or contained, only "within 100 feet of roads, parking areas, and campgrounds." That's typical language, you'll find. That said, there's still fun to be had if you look carefully, especially if you have a small dog. Chloe and I spent a great day on Mount Rainier jnt.im/351, and a Dog Jaunt reader made sure I learned about the options at Yosemite: "Yosemite is the same way — dogs only on paved areas — but then several years ago they paved the trail to Lower Yosemite Fall and didn't change the rules. Plus they closed the paved road to the Tuolumne Grove of Giant Sequoia to cars, which means you can walk down the road with dogs (but you can't leave the road and walk through the grove, which isn't paved). Also, you can walk all over the Valley on paved trails.

The story is much different in national forests and in state parks. In Montana (the home of Yellowstone), for example, dogs are welcome in state parks jnt.im/349 (except in swimming beaches "or any other areas that display posted restrictions"), and in the off-season, your dog can even be off-leash. Montana's national forests have

There are a couple of pet totes that zip closed and will also collapse so they're small enough to fit in a purse or a backpack. My favorite is Target's SportPet jnt.im/101 carrier, which will fit a larger small pet (up to 20 lbs.). It will not stand up to hard use or chewing, but that's not what you're buying it for. In fact, consider buying more than one and stockpiling them for future trips; they're inexpensive, and rare enough that you'll want to have a supply in case they're discontinued.

similar rules (*e.g.,* the Beaverhead-Deer-lodge National Forest jnt.im/350 , in the southwestern corner of the state, and the vast Custer National Forest jnt.im/348). With research jnt.im/347 , you can find stunning scenery to enjoy with your dog.

Ensure that you both have a great day on the trail by carrying plenty of water. A bigger dog can carry some of the load in a dog backpack jnt.im/346 . If the trail is rocky or abrasive, or icy, or if you plan to be hiking all day, protect your dog's feet with boots. If you're hiking on private land, ask about local hunting seasons; to be on the safe side, buy a blaze orange vest jnt.im/345 for your dog.

Speaking of safety, carry your pet first aid kit, or those parts of it you're most likely to need on a hike (including tweezers, clotting agent, Bactine, gauze bandages, and Co-Flex tape). Consider using as your own backpack a carrier that you could pack your pet out in, if need be. Timbuk2's Mutt mover jnt.im/343 is a good choice for small dogs; the Casual Canine Ultimate Backpack Dog Carrier jnt.im/342 is a better fit for larger small dogs like Chloe.

Pack out your dog's poop: It may seem natural, but it poses a risk to wildlife. When you get home, check your dog (and yourself!) for ticks, and carefully remove any you find.

PET-TOGETHERS: DOG PARKS AND MEET-UPS

Chloe and I used to seek out dog parks together when we traveled, but as it's become clearer that she really cares only about squirrels (and sometimes pigeons), we've cut back on our socializing with other dogs and dog owners. Here are some things to keep in mind as you consider your travel exercise options.

DOG PARKS

An off-leash dog park can be a wonderful resource. If your destination has one, it'll be easy to identify on line, and it's a straightforward way to give your dog exercise in an unfamiliar place. It's also a great way to meet other dog owners, and get their recommendations for local care providers and dog-friendly attractions, activities and restaurants. That said, be aware that dog parks can be dangerous places, especially for small dogs, and that you need to look out for potential hazards as you join (even temporarily) a new community.

As you approach a new dog park, try to get a sense of its clientele and cleanliness: Are the dogs interacting? Aggressive? Do their owners seem to be mindful of their whereabouts and behavior?

Take a look, too, at how the dog park is structured. Is the area completely fenced? Are there double gates at the entrance, and are people using them properly? Is there an area set aside for small or older dogs? A dog who is frightened, even momentarily, and yips or squeals may trigger a reaction called "predatory drift jnt.im/341 ," even in normally even-tempered dogs — and a small dog is more likely to be seriously injured in the resulting fracas if bigger dogs are included in the mix.

It's a good idea to bring your own water in a travel water bottle jnt.im/147 , and discourage your dog from using the communal bowl. Another dog may have a disease that can be transmitted through shared water.

To prevent altercations, don't bring treats or toys with you into the dog park.

MEET-UPS

Another way to participate in your destination's pet community is through meet-ups, which can be held at a local park or dog park, or a dog-friendly café or restaurant — or on foot (group walks). From their description, you'll get a sense of the size (often, they're breed-specific) and number of the dogs involved. Meetup jnt.im/344 is a great resource, or search online for "dog meet ups" in the area you're visiting. Here too, leave your dog's treats behind, and when group play becomes too noisy, step in and extract your dog until things calm down.

BIKING WITH YOUR DOG

A special leash that attaches to your bike's frame (e.g., Pet Ego's WalkyDog jnt.im/340, with an optional Low Rider attachment for smaller dogs) allows your dog to run safely alongside you. You will not be able to go far together, since even a larger dog will top out at a couple of miles or so, but very active dogs will appreciate the level of exercise a bike ride delivers.

To make the experience a success, slowly accustom your dog to the leash apparatus and to walking next to your bike, and only gradually add distance to your outings. Bike at a speed that is comfortable for your dog. If you go for a long ride together, give him a day or two off before your next ride. Attach the bike leash to a harness, not a collar. Be very mindful of the condition of your dog's paws, and if you plan a long ride or a ride on a rough or hot surface, equip him with boots. Watch for signs of overheating, and

It is extremely dangerous — for you and your dog, and for pedestrians, runners and other bikers — to use a regular leash to bike with your dog. Unlike a regular leash, a bike leash is designed to help you maintain your balance, and is short enough to keep your dog by your side, not scything down passersby. Even with a bike leash, proceed cautiously while you learn how much space the two of you occupy.

prevent it by putting your dog in a cooling jacket and carrying plenty of water.

At some point (and watch for it), he'll be done with biking for the day. Have an alternative prepared, so you can continue your ride: A dog weighing up to about 20 lbs. jnt.im/339 can be carried in a basket that hangs from the handlebars or attaches to a bracket over your rear wheel (a smaller pet could also be carried in a backpack-style carrier), while a larger dog will need to be pulled in a trailer jnt.im/338.

Your pet, in fact, may prefer to skip straight to the part where he's chauffeured. Check on him from time to time (it'll be a chance for you to catch your breath too) and make sure he's hydrated and protected from the sun.

9

Three pees: Preparation, Paperwork and Packing

This section will help you get your pet ready to travel, and it will point you towards the documents you'll need en route. Carefully selected, good quality gear can make it much easier to travel with your pet: Three packing checklists help you figure out what you'll need, and you'll find advice, too, about keeping all that gear organized and accessible — at home and on the road.

PREPARING YOUR PET FOR TRAVEL

Not every pet is a good traveler. It's up to you to take a careful look at your pet and her personality, social skills and physical condition and decide whether she will comfortably handle the kind of travel you plan to do. If you have concerns, can they be addressed with training, or the help of your veterinarian?

IS YOUR PET A GOOD CANDI-DATE FOR TRAVEL?

Ask yourself these questions:

➤ Is your pet in good physical condition? What kinds of health issues does she have? What level of activity does she prefer?

➤ How comfortable is she around other people, including children?
➤ How comfortable is she around other animals?
➤ Does she have good manners? (In particular, will she walk without pulling? Will she sit on command? Does she have a good recall? Is she house-trained? Does she bark, or chew?)
➤ Does she get motion sickness?
➤ Does she get upset when you leave her alone? How comfortable is she in new environments, like another home, or an office? How does she handle crowds?
➤ Is your dog a kind that is typically targeted by breed bans?

The "wrong" answer need not be a deal-breaker. For example, your pet may have a snub nose and still be a good traveler; you just need to be aware of the breathing and overheating issues brachycephalic pets face, and fly with your Boston Terrier or Himalayan cat only in cabin, and only with input from your veterinarian. If your dog does not currently have good manners, she can acquire them, with your help. With patience and kindly encouragement, a pet prone to motion sickness may become comfortable with travel. Talk to your veterinarian, and consult a skilled and humane trainer, before making a final decision.

MAKING TRAVEL EASIER AND SAFER FOR YOUR PET

If you've reached this paragraph and you're still feeling upbeat, take the next step: Add skills to your pet's repertoire that will make travelling with her easier:

➤ Help your pet learn to enjoy spending time in a crate or carrier. She may be required to be crated during your travels. More positively, a traveling pet may benefit from having access to a familiar and comforting retreat, and crating will keep her safe in certain situations: It's a good solution for large dogs in cars, for example, and a crated dog will not escape your hotel room in your absence.

➤ If your pet isn't already a road warrior, help her learn to be comfortable in a moving car. The same skills will come in handy when you want to take her on a plane.

➤ Teach your dog to use a pee pad. This is particularly helpful for layovers, when an airport's pet relief area is on the land side of security but a family bathroom stall is nearby; it's also a blessing when you'd prefer not to leave your hotel room for that last, late-night walk.

➤ Either learn your dog's signal for when she needs to go outside, or teach her one. One option is to train your dog to use Poochie Bells jnt.im/335, and hang a set on your hotel or guest bedroom door.

➤ Train your dog to eliminate in response to a trigger word or phrase. Chloe's is "hurry up!" and I'll be honest, it means little to her – but many, many dogs are snappier on the uptake than my girl.

For her own health, the health of other creatures, and to satisfy the requirements of entities like other countries, airlines and care providers, your pet will need to have a short list of vaccinations. In addition, talk to your veterinarian about the kinds of nuisances and health hazards your pet may encounter in the region you're visiting and prepare appropriately.

If you live in or anticipate visiting a location where heartworm is prevalent (it's found across the U.S. jnt.im/145, and increasingly in Europe jnt.im/146; it appears to be less common in Australia and New Zealand jnt.im/143, and rare in Tasmania), a product like Revolution, applied to your pet's skin once a month, is advisable. If you live in, or plan to visit, a place where deer ticks (associated with Lyme Disease and potentially not covered by your pet's normal tick control product) are common, ask your vet whether you need to supplement your pet's defenses with Frontline Plus or a tick collar. Lyme Disease is famously found in New England, and also the Upper Midwest, but cases have been reported around the world jnt.im/144.

In many cases, you'll be focusing on a flea, tick and heartworm preventative, but your veterinarian may want to protect your pet against other problems too, depending on your destination.

Not every dog is a traveler, and that's okay. You may already have a friend or relative who yearns to snuggle your dog while you're away; if not, ask questions, do research, and find a good-quality dog camp or hotel for your pup. But have a talk first with your vet and a thoughtful pet trainer (seek out the ones who specialize in "positive reinforcement" training): If you and your pup can work through the issues that worry you, you can hit the road together — and it'll be so much fun you won't want to come back no more, no more, no more.

PAPERWORK

Nearly always, if you're going on a trip with your pet, you'll need some kind of paperwork. It may be as simple as a copy of your pet's shot record, or it may be multiple health certificates, some requiring endorsement by a government agency. This section lets you know how to find out what's needed, and where to go to get the current versions of the documents you'll need.

U.S. INTERSTATE TRAVEL WITH YOUR PET

The federal government takes a hands-off approach `jnt.im/333` to the movement of pets across state lines, leaving it up to the individual states to set their own rules. Nearly all of them `jnt.im/334` require a health certificate for a visiting pet. One exception is California, which only requires that a dog over four months old have a current certificate of rabies vaccination (a rabies vaccination is not required for cats).

All U.S. airlines require a health certificate for a checked or cargo pet, and one (Hawaiian Airlines) requires a health certificate for an in-cabin pet (but only for travel outside the state).

Since it costs about $30 to get a health certificate, if you're flying on a carrier

A health certificate (more formally known as a "Certificate of Veterinary Inspection") is a document signed by a veterinarian, identifying your pet and saying that she is fit to travel and up to date on all of her vaccinations. To get one, you will need to bring your pet to your veterinarian's office, where she'll get a physical exam from the vet, not a technician.

A health certificate is only good for 30 days after your vet signs it, so if your trip will last longer than a month, and a health certificate is needed for your return (or the rest of your itinerary), you'll need to locate a vet and get a new certificate.

other than Hawaiian, do some quick research and see whether your plans are taking you between states that don't have a health certificate requirement. You may decide that even if the states on your itinerary *do* have a health certificate requirement, you'll take the risk of not getting one. I'd be lying if I said I hadn't, myself. After all, where is a request to see your pet's health certificate likely to come from? There are no state representatives waiting to interview you as you step off the plane – and there are no customs officers at state lines, so I don't get a health certificate for road trips either.

The only scenario I can come up with where the topic might arise is if you or your dog created such a ruckus that the police were called in, and they decided to throw the book at you. You're not that kind of traveler, right? Neither am I. That said, I *do* travel with a copy of Chloe's current shot record, and if I owned a pet subject to breed bans or even one that *looks* like one of those pets, I *would* get a health certificate before traveling with her – not because I anticipate that she'll cause trouble, but rather because having a certificate in hand may defuse trouble that is visited upon her.

INTERNATIONAL TRAVEL WITH YOUR PET

Assembling the paperwork and going through the procedures required to take your pet abroad can take just a few days, or it can take weeks. As soon as you have a trip in mind, contact your veterinarian and start working through this checklist:

1. Ask if your veterinarian is USDA-accredited `jnt.im/336` and is comfortable with readying your pet for travel.

If not, get a recommendation to another vet. Whichever vet you choose, make a call to your local USDA office jnt.im/331 to confirm that their accreditation is current.

2. When you make your plane reservations (for you and your pet), think about:
   - The weather — If your pet will be traveling in the baggage or cargo areas, choose a flight that avoids the day's hottest hours and is direct (or has the fewest stops/changes)
   - Layover lengths, and overall travel time — If you have an in-cabin pet, you might consider breaking up a marathon day with a substantial layover that will give her a chance to pee and stretch her legs, or you might seek out the shortest possible direct flight (if you make it an nighttime trip, that'll improve the chances that your pet will sleep during the flight)

3. Ask your airline for any airline-specific requirements, for example:
   - Health certificate
   - Acclimation certificate jnt.im/332
   - A statement from your veterinarian, required by some airlines during cold-weather travel, that your pet can handle temperatures below the range, and for longer than the time period, mandated by the USDA
   - Crate/carrier requirements

4. Learn the import requirements for the country you're visiting.

What if you're just transiting through a country? Typically, documentation for that country will not be required if your pet does not leave the secured part of the airport during your layover. There are important exceptions like, for example, South Africa jnt.im/142, so be sure to research the issue for each of your layovers.

5. Have the required procedures performed, and documents completed, by your USDA-accredited veterinarian. Pay attention to timing! For example:
   - Many countries require that your pet be microchipped before getting her rabies vaccination
   - Some countries require serologic testing (to ensure that your pet's rabies vaccination has done its job) during a certain time frame after vaccination and before arrival; some require that a certain period of time pass after vaccination and before arrival
   - Some countries require tapeworm treatment within a certain time before arrival
   - Your airline may require a health certificate prepared and signed by your vet within 10 days of travel

6. Get USDA endorsement on documents that require it (typically, a country-specific health certificate) at your local USDA office jnt.im/328, either by delivery service or appointment.

7. Call your airline 24-48 hours before departure to confirm your travel plans. Ask about any conditions that might prevent your pet from getting on board

Treat your pet's original, USDA-endorsed documents with the same care you give your own passport! Make several color copies of the packet, so you can give one to an official who wants one, but do not give up the originals. Talk to the USDA office you visit about the issue; they may be able to re-impress their seal on your color copies, so that the copies have the feel, as well as the look, of the original.

with you, including equipment changes, or (if your pet is to travel below) forecasts of extreme temperatures at any of the airports on your route.

GETTING THE INFORMATION YOU NEED FOR THE COUNTRY YOU'RE VISITING

Since not every embassy has up-to-date information and forms, the best place to start is the USDA's page about "International Animal Export Regulations `jnt.im/329`." Scroll down to the "List of Countries" and click on the appropriate letter to find the country you're visiting. (You will also want to read through the USDA's useful section on "Taking Your Pet to a Foreign Country `jnt.im/327`.")

To be doubly sure that you and your vet have the most current rules and forms, call your local USDA office `jnt.im/330`. Ask them for any general tips they have that your vet may not be aware of. For example, your forms should be filled out in blue ink, not black.

The government website of the country you're visiting may contain useful information. You may also want

While there are on-line vendors who sell packets of forms for traveling pets, these too are not always current or complete.

to contact the embassy of each country you're visiting, using the U.S. Department of State's contact information `jnt.im/326`. Be cautious about the information and forms you receive, however, and if you have questions, discuss them with your local USDA office. You will definitely need to contact the embassy or a consulate of the country you're planning to visit if the country is not included in the USDA's list of animal export regulations.

Countries with particularly useful pet import pages include the U.K. `jnt.im/139`, Canada `jnt.im/140`, Australia `jnt.im/138`, New Zealand `jnt.im/137`, Ireland `jnt.im/141`, Italy `jnt.im/135` and Spain `jnt.im/136`. The latter two are in Italian and Spanish (please note that while both pages offer you English versions, clicking on the button will take you to the main, welcome page, and you will have to find your way back to the pet import rules page). Some countries also provide pet importation rules in English through their embassies. The relevant provisions from France's Ministry of Agriculture, Food & Forestry site `jnt.im/133`, for example, are provided in English on its U.S. embassy's page `jnt.im/134`; Germany, too, includes pet import rules on its embassy page `jnt.im/131`, and also provides a link to the relevant page `jnt.im/132` from its Federal Ministry of Food, Agriculture & Consumer Protection site. I recommend looking at both (with the help of Google Translate, if need be), to make sure the embassy pages match what the government agency site says. If you are visiting a country I haven't given you a link for, do a Google search for "[country name] pet import" and look through the results for an official government page.

VISITING COUNTRIES IN
THE EUROPEAN UNION

The requirements for visiting a European Union country (here's the list of current member states jnt.im/323) with a pet differ, and hinge on whether (1) your country is also an EU country; or (2) you are from Andorra, Iceland, Liechtenstein, Monaco, Norway, San Marino, Switzerland or the Vatican; or (3) your country appears on the EU's list of countries with "a favorable situation with regard to rabies;" or (4) your country has "an unfavorable situation" with regard to rabies, or hasn't yet applied to be listed by the EU.

The U.S. is on the list of countries with a favorable situation with regard to rabies jnt.im/324 (see Part C of Annex II, on p. 13-14), so the requirements for bringing a pet to an EU country are:

➤ A 15-digit ISO microchip, implanted before rabies vaccination. U.S. vendors include ResQ, Datamars, HomeAgain (make sure you get the 15-digit chip, since they also offer a 10-digit chip), and Avid (again, make sure you get the Euro chip). If your dog already has a different kind of chip, get your vet to mention it on your pet's health certificate, in case a customs official "sees" a second chip and wonders why it's not responsive.

➤ A rabies vaccination. If this is your pet's first trip to the EU, she must get a rabies vaccination, even if she is currently vaccinated. She may not enter the EU until 21 days after her vaccination. (If you keep her rabies boosters current, there will be no waiting period requirement for future trips to the EU.)

➤ A health certificate filled out by your vet and endorsed by the USDA

➤ Possible additional treatments, depending on the EU country you're visiting. For example, the U.K. jnt.im/321, Ireland jnt.im/322, and Finland jnt.im/319 require that dogs be treated for tapeworm not less than 24 hours and not more than 120 hours (1-5 days) before their arrival. Cats arriving in the U.K. jnt.im/320 from Australia or the Malaysian Peninsula must be accompanied by a certificate showing protection against Hendra disease and Nipah disease, respectively.

That may sound like a lot, but it's a pretty straightforward package to assemble. And once you've met the requirements for one EU country, you've met them for all EU countries. If you want to visit another EU country, your USDA-endorsed health certificate will work until it expires. For example, the French health certificate is good "for a total of 4 months from the date of issue...or until the date of expiry of the anti-rabies vaccination, whichever date is earlier," per Note (e) jnt.im/318.

Alternatively, schedule an appointment with a vet in the first EU country you visit, and have them issue your pet an EU "pet passport jnt.im/325," which lasts for your pet's lifetime. You'll need to show the vet your pet's USDA-endorsed health certificate and her rabies vaccination record, both of which should include her microchip number.

Be sure to have your veterinarian make a note on your pet's passport (or alternative travel documents) with all the details of the tapeworm treatment, including the name and dosage of the medication, and the date and time it was administered.

VISITING THE U.K. WITH A PET: A SPECIAL CASE

While the paperwork for entering the U.K. is the same as that required for entering any other E.U. country (except please note the U.K.'s tapeworm requirement, above), the U.K. is unusual in not allowing pets to arrive in-cabin (your pet is allowed to fly directly to the U.K. in a plane's belly, but only as cargo jnt.im/316). The list of ways a pet is permitted to enter the U.K. jnt.im/317 also includes the Queen Mary 2, several ferry companies jnt.im/315, and private car (carried on the Eurotunnel Le Shuttle jnt.im/314). Please note that private boats and planes are not a viable workaround jnt.im/313.

A workable but expensive option is to fly with your in-cabin pet to Paris or Amsterdam or Brussels (or even Copenhagen or Madrid, though the ferries are pretty distant from both). Schedule an appointment with a local veterinarian for the tapeworm treatment the U.K. requires, and consider, at the same time, getting the vet to convert your pet's paperwork to an E.U. pet passport. Then either make your way to the embarkation point for the ferry you've chosen (please note that not every ferry allows walk-ons), or rent a car and drive to the Pas-de-Calais to board Le Shuttle. Here's where the expense kicks in jnt.im/337: The car rental places that permit one-way rentals into the U.K. add a tremendous surcharge; consider hiring a pet courier jnt.im/308 or, if you're traveling with a companion and have the time, dropping your companion and pet off in England, returning your car to France, and then hopping on the Eurostar to rejoin your traveling companions.

How about flying *out* of the U.K.? The DEFRA pet travel page jnt.im/309, normally a miracle of clarity and thoroughness, only talks about *importing* pets. Logically, there should be no problem with an in-cabin pet leaving the region. It's surprisingly tricky, however, to find an airline that will allow an in-cabin pet to depart the U.K. Your best option is Lufthansa, which took my booking (with Chloe) in stride jnt.im/307, and whose customer service representative firmly assured me that pets can *leave* (but not enter) the U.K. in-cabin on Lufthansa. When you are making your plans, I recommend calling your airline a couple of times to confirm and re-confirm that your pet will be allowed into the cabin, and take good notes each time of the name of the person you spoke to, and the date of your conversation. Alternatively, you can reverse the process that brought you into the U.K. and depart Europe on a flight from the Continent.

VISITING AUSTRALIA AND NEW ZEALAND

Here too, the requirements differ depending on what kind of pet you're proposing to import, and where you will be arriving from. Recall that that pet cats and dogs are not allowed to arrive in-cabin in either Australia jnt.im/310 or New Zealand jnt.im/306, but must rather travel as manifest cargo.

The Australian Quarantine and Inspection Service jnt.im/311 (AQIS) site leads you through the requirements you'll face. Please note that while cats and dogs arriving from New Zealand, the Cocos (Keeling) Islands or Norfolk Island will not be quarantined, all others will, and the quarantine period can be lengthy: A pet

Before you leave Australia with your pet, think about when you will be returning. If you propose returning with your pet within six months of export, consult an AQIS-accredited veterinarian jnt.im/130 (AAV) well before your departure. With preparation, you may be able to avoid an extended stay in quarantine. Please note that if you travel with your pet to a "non-approved country jnt.im/129" like Mongolia, your pet will need to be be tested and vaccinated in an approved country, and exported from there too (though she can spend the intervening months back in Mongolia).

dog arriving from the U.S. (a "Category 3" country) will be quarantined for at least 10 days (per a change to the import policy effective Feb. 3, 2014). The only other pets jnt.im/305 who may be imported into Australia are rabbits and certain birds (but only from New Zealand) and horses.

New Zealand's Ministry of Agriculture and Forestry (MAF) takes a very similar approach to the import of pets. Birds, however, may not be imported into New Zealand jnt.im/312 from any country. The MAF Biosecurity site jnt.im/302 leads you through the process of gathering the documents, test results, and treatments your pet will need, as well as scheduling your pet's stay in quarantine.

RETURNING TO THE U.S.

Pets arriving in the U.S. must meet a short list of federal (and possibly state) requirements:

➤ Under the CDC's rules jnt.im/303, your dog "must have a certificate showing they have been vaccinated against rabies at least 30 days prior to entry"

(not required if your dog has been in a listed rabies-free country for more than 6 months prior to arrival in the U.S.). Please note that cats are not required to have a rabies vaccination certificate. How about other kinds of pets? The Customs and Border Protection agency has a useful summary document jnt.im/301 you'll want to read.

The form of the rabies vaccination certificate is not specified, but should be in English (or be accompanied by a translation). It should identify the animal, the dates of vaccination and expiration, and be signed by a licensed veterinarian. I would also ask the vet to include any identifiers on the label of the vaccine bottle itself.

If you have only spent a brief period abroad, the paperwork you gathered to *export* your dog will likely also work to *import* her; be sure, though, to double-check your expiration dates.

➤ Your pet must be in good health, and may be subject to an inspection if she appears unwell.

➤ If you are arriving from a country affected with screwworm jnt.im/304, you must have a certificate signed by a veterinarian jnt.im/299 stating that your dog has been inspected for screwworm within 5 days prior to shipment to the United States, and that she is either free of screwworm, or was quarantined and treated until free of screwworm.

➤ Officially, too, your dog will need a health certificate if you arrive in a state with a health certificate requirement. Your airline may require a health certificate. What should it include? An example health certificate is provided by the USDA-APHIS jnt.im/300 for your veterinarian's reference. Be sure to read your destination state's requirements carefully, to ensure that the veterinarian addresses all issues of concern.

HOTELS, DAY CARE AND KENNELS

Some hotels may want to see proof that your pet has certain inoculations. Austin's Driskill Hotel `jnt.im/298`, for example, requires "verification of bordetella and rabies vaccinations within the past 12 months." When you make your hotel reservations, find out if you'll need a copy of your pet's current shot record.

If you know that at some point during your trip you'll be leaving your pet in the care of a sitter, or a daycare center or kennel, you should find out what paperwork that provider requires. Typically, they'll require written proof that your dog's vaccinations for rabies, DHPP (Distemper/Hepatitis/Parainfluenza/Parvovirus) and bordetella (kennel cough) are current; a copy of your pet's current shot record should suffice.

Even if you have no current plans to board your pet, consider bringing a current copy of her shot record with you anyway. You simply don't know when the need may arise, and in an emergency, you'll be grateful to have the document you need at your fingertips.

Assembling the correct paperwork is the part of pet travel I find most trying. I handle my concerns by starting early, doing a great deal of reseach, and working with a veterinarian experienced in helping pets get ready for international travel. Work through this chapter, as I do, as soon as you know where your travels will take you next, and you'll be good to go.

SELECTING AND PACKING THE BEST PET TRAVEL GEAR

Even the smallest pet has a mountain of gear. The following are three packing checklists to get you started (essentials, additional useful items, and gear for adventures).

ESSENTIALS

➤ Prescription medications
➤ Anxiety remedies, if needed
➤ Food kit, including food and treats, and bowls for food and water, preferably stainless steel
➤ Water, or a water-purifying solution, if your dog requires it
➤ Travel crate and bedding (pads and/or towels, lengths of polar fleece).
➤ Grooming supplies (*e.g.,* brush, comb, nail clippers, trimmer)
➤ Cleaning supplies (*e.g.,* enzymatic cleaner, paper towels, lint roller)
➤ Sheets, to put over hotel room bed and furniture
➤ Poop-disposal solution: For dogs, extra rolls of poop bags; for pets who use it, litter and a litter box option (for long stays in a vacation rental, consider packing a larger plastic litter box in your suitcase, and packing clothing around it).
➤ An extra leash and harness
➤ Dog water bottle (my favorite is the Gulpy `jnt.im/297`, which also comes in a smaller, 10 oz. size `jnt.im/296`) or collapsible pet bowl `jnt.im/295`
➤ Pet clothing, boots
➤ Safety gear for car travel
➤ Towel or seat cover for car travel
➤ Window shade for car travel
➤ Soft muzzle (sometimes required by trains, ferries, public transit)

➤ Collapsible tote (to carry small
  pets on public transit)

ADDITIONAL USEFUL ITEMS

➤ Toys
➤ Flashlight or headlamp
  for nighttime walks
➤ Dog-walking organizer (arm band,
  clip-on pouch, or waist pack)
➤ Set of Poochie Bells door bells,
  if your dog uses them
➤ Windex wipes (to clean nose
  prints off rental car windows)
➤ Bitter Yuck/Bitter Apple spray,
  especially for puppies
➤ Gaffer's tape or painters' blue tape, to
  tape cables and power cords out of reach
➤ Additional grooming supplies
  (*e.g.*, small bottles of shampoo and
  conditioner; super-absorbent,
  quick-dry microfiber camping
  towels; hair stopper; tub faucet
  adapter; eye and ear cleansing pads;
  pet hair dryer; pet trimmer)
➤ Local dog-oriented guide book
➤ First aid kit

GEAR FOR ADVENTURES

➤ Life jacket/PFD and safety tether
➤ Safety vest or blaze orange handkerchief
➤ Dog backpack (for your dog to wear)
➤ Backpack, tote or sling (to carry
  your small pet); bird owners
  should check out Celltei's many
  backpack options jnt.im/293
➤ Bike carrier or bike leash attachment
➤ Eye goggles (*e.g.*, Doggles jnt.im/294)
➤ Booties for rough or hot surfaces

Include copies of your pet's prescriptions
with your pet's paperwork, so they don't
get lost. And be sure to keep your pet's
medications separate from yours!

These bowls jnt.im/124 in the 1⅓ pint size
work well for a small pet, and fit in our food
kit. I like them because of the non-skid
rubber ring on the bottom. If you have a
metal wire travel crate, consider a water
bowl jnt.im/123 that can be clamped to it.

Crate options for use in a hotel or guest
room include collapsible nylon twill crates
and folding metal wire crates. It is also
possible, though more challenging, to
pack the kind of hard-sided plastic crate
required for checked and cargo pets (of
course, if your pet is traveling in her crate,
packing it is not on your list of concerns).

To preserve your neighbors' sanity, leave
squeaky toys at home. Choose a felt ball,
which is quiet and won't damage hotel walls
or furnishings. If your pup is a ChuckIt fiend
and you anticipate visiting a place where she
can enjoy a game of heave-and-retrieve, the
short-handled ChuckIt! Launcher jnt.im/121
is easier to pack, and is available for use
with both small balls jnt.im/122 and the
standard tennis-sized balls jnt.im/120 .

PACKING YOUR PET'S GEAR

Your goal is to keep all of this gear not
only dry and safe (food and treats, in
particular, need to be preserved from
your pet's between-meals instincts),
but also accessible and organized.

At home, Chloe's gear (grooming
supplies, toys, extra leash and harness,
water bottle, outerwear, etc.) is contained
and organized in an L.L. Bean tote with a

zippered main compartment and several large outer pockets. That particular tote has been discontinued, but a nice alternative is a diaper bag, like the Skip Hop Duo Double `jnt.im/290` diaper bag.

When it's time to travel, the tote goes into our car or, if we're flying, into a suitcase. On car trips, it keeps pet gear organized en route and can easily be carried into hotel rooms. After plane trips, the tote emerges from a suitcase and functions just as it does at home.

PACKING FOOD AND TREATS

Your first instinct will be to put food and treats in resealable bags, and it's a good instinct – but I've learned the hard way that those bags can be pierced by other travel gear, and your pet can smell her food through the seal. I recommend putting the bagged items in a "dry sack" or "dry bag" from a camping or boating supplier (the 8 or 13 liter size, depending on the quantity of food you're packing), along with your travel food and water bowls (I prefer small stainless steel bowls with a rubber bottom), and a folded-up spill mat (a placemat or a length of oilcloth `jnt.im/289`). That way, all of your pet's food-related gear is in one easy-to-grab kit – a blessing when you're trying to feed a hungry pet and your hotel room is a jumble of belongings.

PACKING FOR YOUR OWN CAR

If we are leaving on a road trip in our own car, we pack Chloe's gear in totes. Her 24″ long metal Midwest travel crate and crate pads fit in an extra-large Land's End tote bag `jnt.im/291`, and the many-pocketed storage tote that sits on top of her home crate gets slung in next to it.

PACKING FOR A RENTAL CAR

Packing for this situation is the same as packing for air travel, which I'll turn to next — with one difference. If I know that we'll be driving a rental car at our destination, I pack a car safety solution (for Chloe, it's the Pet Tube `jnt.im/288`) in the suitcase we use to carry Chloe's gear. When we arrive, I install the Pet Tube and its "comfort pillow" in the right rear seat of the rental car, add the extra, soft pad from her in-cabin carrier, insert Chloe, and off we go.

If it'll be a long road trip at our destination, I pull out Chloe's many-pocketed tote and put that on the seat next to her, so it's easily accessible from the front seats and from the driver's side passenger door. Chloe's big suitcase goes in the trunk, to be dealt with when we stop for the night. It's a messy scene in the car rental area while all of this is happening, since I have to open Chloe's suitcase completely, on the ground, to access all the stuff I need, but it only takes a couple of minutes before everything is zipped back up again.

PACKING FOR AIR TRAVEL (CHECKED BAG)

The trickiest part of the process is packing a travel crate for your pup. A crate is an excellent idea for travelers with dogs because many hotels require that your dog be crated while you're absent; in addition, a crate gives your dog a familiar haven as you change environments, and keeps her from bolting out of the room when house cleaning (and the house cleaning cart and vacuum) enters.

If you (unlike me) have a pup that won't shred a soft-sided crate, you're lucky, because they're compact and lighter than the metal wire crate I pack for Chloe. I recommend the Creature Leisure soft-sided Ultimate Dog Den crate `jnt.im/287`; the medium size that works well for Chloe also fits in a large suitcase (which can itself be soft-sided, in this case). Please note that Creature Leisure makes a version of its Dog Den for another company, Bergan `jnt.im/292`. An argument *against* a soft-sided crate is that you can't attach a water bowl `jnt.im/284` to it, as you can to a metal wire crate. You can, of course, put a water bowl in with your pet, but it may tip over.

If you like to use the hard-sided plastic PetMate Sky Kennel your pet flies in for her at-home crate as well, you can either leave it assembled and check it like a suitcase (I recommend packing only light, bulky things in it), or you can unscrew its sides and pack the top and bottom, nested together, *in* a suitcase. This is, of course, assuming that she's not traveling in it herself!

We use a metal Midwest crate for Chloe, and the one she has at home is 30" long. I initially thought I'd be packing it up each time we traveled, so I bought a 32" suitcase to hold it `jnt.im/285`. I chose a hard-sided suitcase, because the edges of the metal wire crate would wreak havoc on a soft-sided suitcase (which, in turn, wouldn't protect the crate from airline baggage handling). Because I wanted the hard-sided suitcase to be as light as possible, I ended up buying the phenomenally expensive Samsonite Cosmolite 32" Spinner `jnt.im/283` suitcase, in red. I've never regretted it: It's light, it's sturdy, it's easy to wheel around, and it's impossible to miss coming off the baggage claim belt.

Please note that if your everyday, many-pocketed organizational tote is bursting at the seams, you can purchase a second, smaller tote to carry just the gear your pet needs for travel (rather than *all* of her toys, and *both* of the fanny packs you use for dog-walking, and all *three* of her water bottles, etc.). That makes packing even easier, because that fully-stocked travel tote can live in your pet's suitcase between trips.

I did change my mind about the crate, however. We pack the next smaller size instead `jnt.im/286` (24" long), which keeps the weight down and leaves room around its edges for Chloe's soft furnishings.

The more you travel, the more routine this packing job will become. Between trips, I leave most of Chloe's gear in the Big Red Suitcase, so that when the time to pack arrives, all I have to do is grab the tote that rests on her home crate (keeping her everyday gear organized), put it into the XL Ziploc bag, fill the food kit with the appropriate amount of food and treats, and place both — along with Chloe's messenger bag and her Pet Tube — in the zipped side of the suitcase.

PACKING FOR AIR TRAVEL (IN-CABIN)

Although some U.S. `jnt.im/280` and international `jnt.im/281` airlines may allow you to board with a carry-on as well as your pet's carrier, many don't. What if your pet's suitcase doesn't end up at your destination at the same time you do? Here is a list of the gear I carry into the cabin with me:

➤ A couple of meal's worth of food (either a small sack of her kibble, or one or two of the tiniest Natural Balance dog food rolls jnt.im/282)

- ➤ Extra-good treats, to coax her back in her carrier en route
- ➤ A collapsible water bowl
- ➤ A water bottle (filled once I'm past security)
- ➤ Leash and harness, for unfenced pet relief areas
- ➤ Poop bags
- ➤ Health certificate (if needed) and a current copy of Chloe's shot record
- ➤ Prescription medications
- ➤ Picture of your dog jnt.im/279
- ➤ Battery-powered fan

How do I do that when an airline's rules prohibit me from bringing a carry-on with me? I pack the gear in my "small personal item" (in my case, a robustly-sized purse), in the pocket of Chloe's in-cabin carrier, or tucked into one of the many pockets in my travel vest jnt.im/278 . I strongly recommend a many-pocketed vest for travelers with dogs, since your small personal item has to go in the overhead bin, and on bumpy flights you may never be allowed to access it.

I have a passion for dog travel gear that you may not share, but that works to your advantage. I buy *all* the things so that I can recommend the *best* things to you. This chapter gathers together the products that have worked well for me over the years I've traveled with Chloe, and I believe they'll make your life (and your dog's life) easier while you're traveling together.

HERE'S WHAT CHLOE'S SUITCASE CONTAINS, ON A TYPICAL TRIP:

Open side, from bottom to surface

- ➤ Quick-dry camping towels (filling in the indents between the channels for the suitcase's handle)
- ➤ Nylon-twill-over-foam crate pad, about 1.5" thick
- ➤ 24" Midwest single-door crate
- ➤ Two (one, if I'm packing Chloe's Pet Tube) soft crate pads
- ➤ Two sheets and a larger camping towel that I use mostly as a crate cover, rolled up and inserted around the three outer edges of the crate

Zipped side

- ➤ Chloe's many-pocketed tote, the entire thing inserted into an extra-large resealable zippered storage bag jnt.im/128 to corral the small bits and protect against liquid (shampoo, enzymatic cleaner, etc.) leakage
- ➤ Chloe's food kit
- ➤ Chloe's large Pet Ego messenger bag
- ➤ Pet Tube and comfort pillow (if car travel at the destination is planned)

Even fully loaded, the Big Red Suitcase has always squeaked in at just under 50 lbs. You could, conceivably, divide your pet's gear between your suitcase and that of a companion, obviating the need for a separate pet suitcase, but I've never managed to be that efficient.

10

Troubleshooting

You started thinking about your pet's health and safety on the road when you asked yourself about his physical characteristics and condition, and his personality and training. This chapter offers strategies for dealing with concerns you may have and highlights issues you may face.

MOTION SICKNESS AND ANXIETY

How can you tell if your pet has motion sickness? He'll look uncomfortable, and he may move around restlessly, lick his lips, pant, whine, yawn and drool a lot. Vomiting, of course, is unmistakable. Motion sickness is largely an issue for younger pets, whose inner ear structures are still developing, but it can be a problem if a dog or cat learns while young to associate car rides with internal uneasiness.

Immediate solutions include opening a window, and stopping the car and taking a walk. A small dog may do better in a booster seat, so he can see out the window. Take short trips (preferably at a slow pace, on flat roads without dramatic turns) to fun places, like a dog park, or a favorite pet store, so your dog learns that car trips have happy endings. Try limiting your pet's food before getting in the car, and giving him a high-quality toy or chew once he's in the car. And if the problem persists, consult your vet, who may prescribe an anti-nausea medication like Cerenia; a few symptom-free trips may help your pet regard your car in a new light.

If you have an anxious pet, you may not know the precise source of his unhappiness. It may have sprung from early, bad experiences with motion sickness, or it may have another cause. All you know is that your pet is desperately unhappy — scratching, whining, barking — in a crate, or in a carrier, or in the car. Work very gradually toward your goal. If you want your pet to be comfortable in a carrier, start by leaving it out, open, on your floor. Make it temptingly comfortable, with soft bedding and a favorite toy. Throw treats in it. Put his food bowl in its opening, and then further in. Zip him in only briefly, then immediately let him out. Slowly increase the amount of time that you keep him zipped in. Pick him up in the carrier, then put it down and let him out. Pick him up, walk around, and then let him out. In short, divide your ultimate goal (putting him, in his carrier, in your car for a trip) into a series of small, achievable steps, shower him with praise and high-quality treats, and make sure he's comfortable with each step before progressing.

There are a number of products that may help. People have reported success with herbal remedies like Rescue Remedy jnt.im/273 (a few drops in your pet's water, or rubbed on a paw or an ear) and Travel Calm jnt.im/274 or lavender essence (spritzed in your dog's carrier). D.A.P., short for "Dog Appeasing Pheromone," mimics the pheromones that female dogs secrete while nursing. A spritz in your dog's carrier jnt.im/272 may lessen her anxiety; it also comes as a TSA-friendly wipe jnt.im/275 you can use on your dog's travel carrier and in a collar jnt.im/271 (the link is to the small size) we've used on Chloe with, I think, some success. Feliway is the feline equivalent, and it's available in diffusers jnt.im/276, for hotel room use, and a spray jnt.im/269.

Try buying your anxious dog a Thundershirt jnt.im/270, which applies gentle pressure around your dog's torso (like swaddling an unhappy baby). Your dog may respond well to the Through A Dog's Ear jnt.im/267 albums of calming music, played to him over your iPhone or iPod (set the volume low and tuck the player into a pocket of his carrier, so only he can hear the music). Please note that both of these options require some advance work; neither will work at their best if you spring them on your pup the day of travel.

If none of these over-the-counter remedies helps, talk to your vet about an anti-anxiety prescription. Tranquilizers are not recommended for pets traveling in the hold, since they affect your pet's breathing and balance. Even for your in-cabin pet, they may be a poor idea. That said, your vet may suggest a tranquilizer, and if so, rely on her to select a medication and dosage appropriate for your pet's age and condition.

PETS WITH SPECIAL NEEDS

If your pet is older, he may take longer to adjust to a new environment. Help him by packing favorite toys and bedding that smells like home. Ensure that you have enough of the food he's used to, or can buy more of it at your destination. Give him time to get over jet lag, if you're in a new time zone: Take shorter, leisurely walks, and make them frequent, too, in case the time difference has thrown off his inner workings. Keep him hydrated.

Work closely with your vet as you plan to travel with your diabetic pet. A road trip can be workable jnt.im/268, since you'll have room to pack the gear you'll need, and the flexibility to stop when your pet's schedule requires it. Shorter plane trips, involving a limited time zone change, and to an area well supplied with veterinary hospitals (in case of emergency), may be possible for your pet. Remember to declare to the TSA officials that you're traveling with insulin, and bring a copy of your pet's prescriptions for insulin and needles with you. Keep the insulin chilled with cold packs, and prevent it from being shaken or jostled heavily. Pack food and Karo syrup in your carry-on. You may also want to pack all, or many, of the testing supplies you anticipate needing, in case your checked luggage is lost. Insulin adjustments should be made only slowly, so you'll want to shift your schedule no more than an hour a day. On balance, and given the uncertainties of air travel, you and your vet may decide that your pet should only fly when it's absolutely necessary.

BREED BAN PETS

Certain dogs will find it harder to travel because their breed is considered potentially dangerous by an airline (e.g., Continental/United Airlines jnt.im/266, Air France jnt.im/277, Virgin Atlantic jnt.im/262, Qantas jnt.im/263, and others), or a hotel or campground, or a municipality (e.g., Denver jnt.im/261, Ontario jnt.im/264), or a country (e.g., the U.K. jnt.im/258). The breeds most often listed are Pit Bull Terriers, American Staffordshire Terriers, Rottweilers and Mastiffs. Owners of Doberman Pinschers, Rhodesian Ridgebacks, German Shepherds, Akitas, American Bulldogs, Huskies, Shar-Pei and Chow Chows have experienced problems with breed bans. In some cases, the ban extends to dogs whose genetic mix includes a banned breed, or who *look* like a banned breed dog.

The consequences can be serious jnt.im/259, including impoundment, fines, and, potentially, euthanization. If you own a dog that has appeared on one of these lists, research your itinerary before you leave and steer around destinations with breed bans. Carry a muzzle, in case you encounter an unexpected local rule requiring them, and consider getting (and carrying proof of) liability insurance.

Even where there is no breed ban, owners of dogs from breeds with PR problems should think about the image their dog projects. A pink bandana and flowery leash on your Pit Bull is a good indicator that your dog is a sweetheart. Alternatively, if you'd prefer that people give your dog some space, consider putting a soft muzzle on him; a clever option from Oppo jnt.im/257 is a muzzle shaped like a duck's bill, which both serves the basic purpose of a muzzle and sends the message that your pup has issues but isn't a monster. Consider a leash from FriendlyPetCollars jnt.im/260: The bright colors and easy-to-read text are

Please note that other pets are also subject to bans. For example, owning a ferret is illegal in California and Hawaii (and in many other smaller U.S. jurisdictions) and in several countries (including Portugal and New Zealand), and owning a gerbil is illegal in California jnt.im/119. If your pet is not a cat or a dog, do some research to make sure he'll be welcome at your destination and in the places you pass through en route.

eye-catching and informative. The clearer the signals you send, the less likely it is that someone will unnerve your dog by treating him in a way you don't expect.

FEEDING YOUR PET AWAY FROM HOME

Even if your pet has an iron stomach, you'll want to travel with food he's familiar with. Ideally, you'd pack all of the food he'll need. On a longer trip, you may not have the luggage room. In that case, research whether you can buy your pet's preferred food at the location you're visiting. If not, you might ship yourself a package of his food. If your dog can handle change, gradually shift to a brand that is available at your destination, either before you leave or once you're there (using the supply you brought of his original food to make the transition).

If your dog is on a raw diet, you can ship yourself, at tremendous expense, a supply of fresh raw food in dry ice, or you can shop for the ingredients at your destination. Be warned that a fresh raw diet is very hard to pull off in a hotel, now that minibars are becoming extinct, but is certainly workable if you're visiting friends or family. Simpler alternatives include freeze-dried or dehydrated raw food (*e.g.*, ZiwiPeak, Stella & Chewy's, Honest Kitchen), which combine nearly all of the purported advantages of a raw diet with portability.

What if your dog demands home cooking? On the road, order (at a restaurant, or from room service) a plain burger, plain rice, and plain vegetables, and mix them together for your dog. The items on a children's menu are more likely to be simple, and therefore easier on your dog's stomach. Look for toddler food at the local grocery store: One seasoned traveler reports that Gerber Graduates "meat sticks" and beef and chicken stews pleased her picky dog `jnt.im/265` and were readily available.

Some very sensitive pets may react poorly to a change in the water they drink. If so, you can pack a quantity of the water your pet's used to. Unless you're driving, though, that's going to be a daunting task. You could pack enough water in your suitcase to make a gradual transition to your destination's water — but what if you're going to multiple destinations? Consider giving your sensitive dog filtered water (*e.g.,* from a Brita pitcher) at home, and carrying a filter device like the Brita Bottle `jnt.im/253` with you, to improve the chance that he won't notice differences in the water he receives. Experiment with shorter trips before taking that month-long trip around Eastern Europe you're planning.

CLOTHING FOR DEMANDING WEATHER

Before you leave, research the weather you're likely to have, and pack any clothing your dog may need. Not every dog needs an extra layer when it's cold, but a short-haired or older pet will appreciate a fleece jacket `jnt.im/254`, a sweater, or even a puffy jacket `jnt.im/252`. Dogs who dislike rainy walks may be persuaded outdoors, or will stay out longer, in a rain jacket `jnt.im/255`. If you expect hot weather, pack a cooling jacket that refreshes in cold water.

Thin rubber booties `jnt.im/256` may look silly, but they're a cheap and easy way to help your dog handle sidewalk salt and packing snow. Sturdier boots `jnt.im/248` will help your hiking buddy on rocky trails and beaches, or on ice or hot asphalt.

PREPARING FOR MEDICAL EMERGENCIES

With some modest groundwork, you can put yourself and your pet in a good position to respond to a medical emergency away from home.

If your pet is taking prescription medications, ensure that you have a sufficient quantity for your entire trip, plus a few days' extra, in case your return is delayed. Carry a copy of the prescription with you; a TSA or customs official may ask to see it.

Identify a good veterinarian and an emergency clinic at your destination. In the United States, the American Animal Hospital Association has a searchable directory of AAHA-accredited veterinarians `jnt.im/249`, and the Veterinary Emergency and Critical Care Society has a searchable directory of emergency clinics `jnt.im/247`.

In other countries, a good place to start is the AngloInfo `jnt.im/250` website, focused on Americans living abroad. Choose your destination, then look under "Family Life & Living" for the "Dogs, Cats, Pets & Animals" subcategory. You'll typically find several veterinary practices listed, and sometimes an emergency clinic (if not, write an e-mail message to one of the listed veterinarians and ask how you should handle an emergency, if the need arises). Take a look at user review sites like Yelp and Citysearch for more details about the listings you get, and for additional suggestions. Your host or the hotel at your destination may also be able to point you to a good local veterinarian and emergency clinic; alternatively, call a pet store at your destination and ask for a recommendation. For extra points, program the vet's and clinic's contact information into your phone.

Add to your phone the number for the ASPCA Animal Poison Control Center: 1-888-426-4435. A doctor will answer your call, and they're open around the clock.

Ask your vet for a copy of your pet's medical file, scan it, and store the data on a USB flash drive (or "thumb drive"). That way, her entire record is at your fingertips — no waiting for a fax from your vet. If you have email on your phone, mail it to yourself as an attachment so you can readily find and forward it when needed.

Talk to your vet (and do some research of your own) about possible medical hazards your pet may encounter at your destination, and deal with them proactively. For example, if you plan to visit Southern Europe with your dog, your vet may send you with a tick collar or other preventative to handle not only ticks but also leishmaniasis (the Scalibor collar is often mentioned, but discuss with your vet reports of adverse reactions).

If your itinerary will take you someplace out of easy reach of a veterinarian, pack a first aid kit. How elaborate it is will depend on how long it might take you to get to a veterinarian, what kind of activities you're planning, and what part of the world you'll be in. A fairly complete kit can be purchased from L.L. Bean jnt.im/246 (I'd add a clotting agent and a muzzle), or you can assemble your own. Here are two lists, of first aid basics, and additional useful items (conveniently, most of these items are also useful for humans).

BASIC PET FIRST AID KIT

➤ Pet thermometer (if you choose a digital thermometer, be sure to pack a fresh battery for it, unless it comes with a long-lasting lithium battery)

➤ Roll of gauze bandage (wrap wound, staunch blood, improvise muzzle)

➤ Package of gauze squares (pad wound, staunch blood)

➤ Celox granule packets jnt.im/251 or PetClot (25g) sponge jnt.im/244 (clotting agent)

➤ Roll of self-sticking Co-Flex bandaging tape (hold pads to wound, hold splint to limb)

➤ Disposable cold pack (reduce swelling)

➤ Bottle of hydrogen peroxide (induce vomiting)

➤ Activated charcoal tablets (absorbs some poisons)

➤ Dropper (administer hydrogen peroxide)

➤ Muzzle

➤ Disposable razor (shave fur around wound)

➤ First Aid guide

ADDITIONAL USEFUL ITEMS

➤ Hydrocortisone spray
➤ Bactine
➤ Benadryl tablets
➤ Noxema
➤ Solarcaine spray
➤ Children's Pepto Bismol tablets
➤ Immodium tablets
➤ Milk of Magnesia
➤ Clotrimazole cream
➤ Baby aspirin (enteric-coated)
➤ Pill splitter
➤ Scissors
➤ Q-tips and cotton balls
➤ Saline eye wash preparation
➤ Tweezers
➤ Elizabethan collar

Make a list of the kit's contents, noting expiration dates for perishable products, and package them and the list in a large resealable zippered storage bag to keep everything organized and visible. Be sure to check the expiration dates from time to time to keep your kit current.

ENSURING THAT YOUR LOST PET IS RETURNED TO YOU

The prospect of losing your pet is particularly horrifying in a location where you're unfamiliar with the local resources and, potentially, the language. If you take a few precautions before you leave, you'll be able to respond promptly and effectively in a crisis, and you'll make it easier for your pet to be restored to you.

Start by microchipping your pet. Commercial interests have unnecessarily complicated jnt.im/243 the available chip choices in the United States. If you live outside the U.S., your best choice is a 15-digit, 134.2 kHz, ISO-compliant chip (*e.g.,* ResQ, Datamars). If you live in the U.S., think about where you're located and where you plan to travel. The 9-digit, 125 kHz chip is still most common in the U.S., and a shelter (especially outside metropolitan areas) may have a scanner that detects only those chips. The 15-digit chips are spreading rapidly, though, so if you live in a metropolitan area (and especially if you plan to travel abroad), you could choose to get just a 15-digit chip. If you live in, or plan to visit, a more rural area, you could choose to stick with a 9-digit chip, and add a 15-digit chip if you go abroad.

Your next line of defense is your dog's ID tag, and here you have a wealth of options. I've tried, or Dog Jaunt readers have tried, the following approaches:

> Each time your pet goes in for his annual check-up, have your vet make sure his chip is still transmitting, and is still located in his shoulder-blade region (chips can migrate). Double check with your pet's chip company to make sure your contact information is current.

➤ Your dog's tag includes the URL of a dedicated website, with contact information for you (which you can update at will, as you travel) and medical information for your pet (in case he needs medical attention while he's in a stranger's hands).

➤ Instead of a dedicated website, the tag has an e-mail address on it jnt.im/242. When a rescuer writes to that address, they receive an automatic response with details about the pet's needs and how to contact his owner; at the same time, a message is automatically sent to the owner, alerting them that their pup has been found.

➤ The tag is printed with a QR code, to be scanned with a phone (there are several free code reader apps) by your pet's rescuer. Buy a QR tag or collar from PetHub jnt.im/245, or make one yourself jnt.im/240.

➤ The blanketID jnt.im/241 tag, a very attractive option, is marked with a unique number; when you go to the maker's site and type in the tag number, you're given the pet owner's contact information and the pet's medical information. The owner, meanwhile, can go to the site and print a "lost pet" poster immediately, using the same (or edited) information, and the service will send it to all nearby animal shelters and hospitals (U.S. and Canada only).

Since a simple phone call may be sufficient to reunite pet and owner (and since not everyone has a smart phone, or immediate access to the Internet), your pet's tag should also include your cell phone number (so a call will reach you even when you're traveling). If you've chosen a tag that doesn't give you the option of providing your phone number, consider getting your pet a collar that has your phone number woven into it jnt.im/238.

If you do not choose a tag that includes a poster-making option, be sure to carry with you several pictures of your pet, clearly showing his markings, so that you can make an effective "lost pet" poster for him. Remember that your poster will need to be in the local language: Google Translate jnt.im/239 isn't perfect, but it will get the job done.

As soon as you have a poster in hand, fax it to all local shelters, animal hospitals and animal control offices. Place a missing pet notice on Craigslist. Post copies of your poster in the neighborhood where your pet went missing. Make smaller versions and tuck them under windshields and doormats. Visit all nearby shelters in person, daily (your fax is an important first step, but you want to ensure it's not overlooked; your pet, too, may arrive looking different from his picture). If you are unfamiliar with the local animal rescue resources, ask for help and advice at a nearby veterinarian's office.

NO FAUX PAWS: BEING A RESPONSIBLE PET OWNER

The previous sections of this chapter have addressed specific problems; this one, instead, points out some general things you can do to make traveling with your dog not only safe but fun. We all want to be met with an open-hearted welcome, and that's where "petiquette" comes in.

The thing to keep in mind, always, is that for owners of service animals, pet travel is a right; for other travelers, it's a privilege, and still a fragile one. Business owners will keep adding pet-friendly amenities if they see that the benefits to them outweigh the disadvantages — keep the scale tilting in the right direction by being a good traveler and a good guest. The essence of good manners is being considerate of others, but here are some specific things you can do to make traveling with your dog a joy:

➤ Work with your dog and a trainer to ensure that she mixes well with people, including children, and other dogs. She should not jump, and she should have a solid "sit" command and recall. She should walk by you, or near you, without pulling.

➤ If your dog has issues she's still working through, protect her and others by sending clear signals that she should not be approached. Put out your hand in a stop gesture, back away, call out an explanation (cheerfully, but firmly) — do whatever it takes to make an enthusiastic human or dog understand that your dog needs space.

➤ Be aware that there are people who fear and dislike dogs, even a pup as harmless as Chloe (and a more harmless dog has never been born). I was surprised to learn that small children are often wary of dogs. There are, too, people who are desperately allergic to pet dander. Do not assume that everyone you meet will be delighted by your delightful pup, and do your best to understand that from their point of view, given their history or issues, their reaction is reasonable. It will put a momentary damper on your day to encounter someone who reacts poorly to your dog, but respect their point of view (and assist them by keeping her from approaching them) — and soothe yourself by remembering the fifty previous happy encounters you've had.

➤ Always ask if your dog is welcome before entering a business establishment (for bonus points, offer to carry her in your arms). If she is, express your thanks enthusiastically (for bonus points, buy something). If not, express your regret politely. If you want to relieve your vexation, a harmless way to do it is to mention how much you had been looking forward to shopping/staying in/otherwise spending money in the off-limits establishment.

➤ When you and your dog are outside your home, interacting (or potentially interacting) with other creatures, be focused on her and your surroundings. If you need to make or take a call, find a quiet place to one side and focus on your phone. Multitasking, when you have a dog with you, leads to all kinds of faux paws (including poop that you fail to pick up) or worse (including inappropriate or dangerous interactions with people or other dogs). Add in a retractable leash, and you have a recipe for disaster: A moment's inattention, and your dog may be out in traffic.

➤ Speaking of poop, always carry poop bags with you, and use them. In an urban environment, dog waste is an eyesore and a source of irritation, and in any environment it poses a health hazard to humans and wildlife. If your pup makes a mess indoors, have the materials with you (packet of folded paper towels, small bottle of enzymatic cleaner, poop bag) to clean up. Do your best to avoid accidents by giving her a good walk before heading inside.

If by now you're having palpitations, know that you are not alone. I am a world-class worrier. I handle my concerns by imagining worst-case scenarios ahead of time, and then preparing for them. This chapter touches on the main concerns people have about traveling with their pet — if yours is not listed, let me know and we'll fret about it (and prepare for it!) together. Anticipating a problem, and addressing it ahead of time, will let you and your pup really enjoy your jaunt.

Airline Policies

I created the following four charts for my blog, Dog Jaunt, to give travelers an overview of the major U.S. and international airlines' pet policies for both in-cabin and checked pets.

This information changes frequently, and often without notice. I update the charts periodically, and when I update them for the blog I will also update them here. Your copy of this book, however, may have been printed just before an update, so your charts' details may be imperfect. Please go to dogjaunt.com to see the most current versions (when you do, you will find that the names of the airlines are links to those airlines' pet policies, giving you quick access to details).The following information has been collected from the airlines' published pet policies, supplemented (in some cases) by telephone inquiries. It was last updated on April 16, 2013.

For each airline, I have provided a link to the airline's pet policy. Please note that the policies include details that I can't fit into this chart. For example, some countries do not allow pets to arrive in-cabin (including the U.K., South Africa and Australia). Because of airplane cabin configurations, in-cabin pets won't fit at all under some sections' seats. Information like this varies by airline, so read the policies carefully. If you still have questions, call your airline's contact number and get answers before you arrive at the airport.

It is also a good idea to print out a copy of your airline's policy, so that if a dispute arises with a ticketing or gate agent, you will have the actual policy to refer to (not the agent's potentially faulty memory of the policy).

U.S. IN-CABIN PET TRAVEL

Airline	Pets in cabin	Pets per passenger	Weight limit	Minimum age	Carrier size	Fee (each way)
AirTran	6	1	none	none	8.5Hx18.5Lx13.5W	$75 ($95 after 1/15/14)
Alaska	1 in First 5 in Coach	1 (note A)	none	8 weeks	7.5Hx17Lx12W hardsided 9.5Hx17Lx12W softsided	$100
Allegiant	no limit	1 carrier, max. 2 pets	none	none	9Hx19Lx16W	$100
American	2 in First 5 in Coach	1 carrier (note B)	20 lbs. total	8 weeks	9Hx19Lx13W (slightly larger if soft-sided)	$125
American Eagle, American Connection	2	1 carrier (note B)	20 lbs. total	8 weeks	9Hx19Lx13W	$125
Continental	same as United					
Delta	2 in First 4 in Coach	1 carrier (note C)	none	10 weeks	varies, call Reservations (800-221-1212)	$125 (North America); $200 (international except $75 to/from Brazil)
Frontier	10 carriers	1 carrier (note D)	none	none	to fit under-seat space measurements	$75 or $125 (depending on fare option)
Hawaiian	5 total (B-717); 2 in First, 5 in Coach (B-767 and A330)	1 (note E)	25 lbs. total	8 weeks	9.5Hx16Lx10W	$35 inter-island; $175 leaving HI; not allowed to arrive in HI
JetBlue	"limited number"	1	20 lbs. total	none	8.5Hx17Lx12.5W	$100
Southwest	6 carriers	1 carrier (note F)	none	8 weeks	to fit under-seat space measurements	$75 ($95 after 1/15/14)

Airline	Pets in cabin	Pets per passenger	Weight limit	Minimum age	Carrier size	Fee (each way)
Spirit	4 carriers	1 carrier (note G)	none	8 weeks	5Hx18Lx14W	$100
Sun Country	4 in plane, with no more than 2 in First	1	16 lb. pet	none	8Hx16Lx11W softsided only	$125 (advance "conditional" reservation); $199 (walk-up)
United	1 in First/Business if space allows, 4 in Economy	Not stated	none	8 weeks	7.5Hx17.5Lx12W hardsided 11Hx18Lx11H softsided	$125 (North America; prices vary abroad)
U.S. Air	not stated	1	none	none	3Hx17Lx16W hardsided 10Hx17Lx 6W softsided U.S. Air Express varies by plane	$125
Virgin America	not stated	1	20 lbs. total	8 weeks	8Hx18Lx15W	$100

NOTES

A. "A customer may travel with a maximum of two (2) pet carriers in the main cabin, only when the adjacent seat is purchased by the same customer." (Alaska)

B. "Only one pet kennel per ticketed passenger may be accepted for travel in the cabin… If two animals are traveling in the same carrier, they must be the same species (two cats or two dogs, not one of each) and the pet and container can weigh no more than 20 lbs. combined." (American)

C. "Two pets of the same species and size may be allowed to travel in one kennel, provide they are small enough to fit into one kennel and are compatible. They will be charged as one pet." (Delta)

D. "Up to two (2) small animals may be transported in one travel container as follows: puppies or kittens (8-10 weeks old), hamsters, guinea pigs, rabbits, and small household birds." (Frontier)

E. 1 container per customer; 1 adult pet per container. "Up to two (2) puppies, or two (2) kittens at least 8 weeks, but no more than 6 months, may be carried in one (1) kennel, provided they do not exceed a total weight of 25 pounds." (Hawaiian)

F. "Southwest Airlines allows only one pet carrier per ticketed Customer. The carrier may contain two (2) cats or dogs and must be of the same species per carrier."

G. "A maximum of 2 pets per container is permitted, but only one container per customer is allowed." (Spirit)

INTERNATIONAL IN-CABIN PET TRAVEL

Airline	Pets in cabin	Pets per passenger	Weight limit	Minimum age	Carrier size	Fee (each way)
Aer Lingus	No (checked or cargo only)					
Aeroflot	Yes	1	8 kg (18 lbs.) total	not stated	"115 cm in three dimensions (length, height, width)"	calculated as excess baggage
AeroMexico	Yes (dogs only, on flights 5 hours or less)	1	9 kg total (7 kg total on E-145 planes)	8 weeks	16Lx12Wx7H (E-145 planes) or 19Lx12Wx10H (all other planes)	not stated
Air Canada	Yes	1	10 kg (22 lbs.) total	8 weeks	21.5Lx15.5Wx9H (if soft-sided, can be 10.5" tall)	$50 or $100 CAD (depending on destination)
Air France	Yes	not stated	6 kg (13.2 lbs.) total	15 weeks (8 weeks in "metropolitan France")	not specified; the carrier Air France sells is 46x28x27cm	200 from/to USA (EUR, USD or CAD, depending on country of departure)
Air New Zealand	No (checked or cargo only)					
Alitalia	Yes	up to 5 (note A)	10 kg total	not stated	17.5x8.5Wx10.2H (40x20x24 cm)	$260 from USA; 200 to USA (EUR, USD or CAD, depending on country of departure)
American Airlines	Yes (Canada, Mexico, Central America, Colombia, and the Caribbean)	1 kennel (note B)	20 lbs. total	8 weeks	19Lx13Wx9H (slightly larger ok if soft-sided)	$125

Airline	Pets in cabin	Pets per passenger	Weight limit	Minimum age	Carrier size	Fee (each way)
ANA All Nippon Airways	No (checked only)					
Asiana Airlines	Yes	1	5 kg total	8 weeks	"The height of the case shall not exceed 21cm (25cm for soft cases)."	calculated as excess baggage
British Airways	No (cargo only)					
Cathay Pacific Airlines	No (checked or cargo only)					
Continental	same as United					
Delta	Mostly (note H)	1 (note C)	not stated	10 weeks	varies by plane; call Reservations	200; 75 for Brazil (EUR, USD or CAD, depending on country of departure)
Emirates	No (checked or cargo only)					
Etihad	No (cargo only)					
EVA Air	No (checked only)					
Iberia	Yes	not stated	8 kg total	not stated	"The container may be a maximum of 45 cm in length, 35 cm in width and 25 cm in depth, provided that the sum of those 3 measurements does not exceed 105 cm."	calculated as excess baggage

Airline	Pets in cabin	Pets per passenger	Weight limit	Minimum age	Carrier size	Fee (each way)
Icelandair	No (checked or cargo only)					
JAL	No (checked or cargo only)					
KLM	Yes	1	5 kg (13 lbs.) total	not stated	A hard-sided container no more than 20 cm tall	20-200 (EUR, USD or CAD, depending on destination and country of departure)
Korean Air	Yes	1 (note E)	5 kg (11 lbs.) total	8 weeks	"The total dimension (length + width + height) of the kennel should not exceed 115 cm to fit under the seat."	calculated as excess baggage
LAN	No (checked or cargo only)					
Lufthansa	Yes	1	8 kg total	not stated	55 cm x 40 cm x 23 cm	$100 USD/CAD, 70€(intercontinental)
Open Skies	Yes	1	6 kg (13.2 lbs.) total	not stated	not stated	$196 or 125€
Qantas	No (checked or cargo only)					
Qatar Airways	No (checked or cargo only)					
Ryanair	No (see Section 8.9.1)					
SAS	Yes	1	8 kg total	not stated	40 cm x 25 cm x 23 cm	$125 or 100€ (intercontinental)

Airline	Pets in cabin	Pets per passenger	Weight limit	Minimum age	Carrier size	Fee (each way)
Singapore Airlines	No (checked or cargo only)					
Swiss	Yes	1	8 kg total	not stated	"Length + width + height = max. 118 cm"	$100 USD/CAD to Europe (plus CHF 88 customs fee if you fly directly to Switzerland); 70€ from Europe to USA; CHF 90 from Switzerland to USA
TAP Portugal	Yes	1 carrier (note F)	8 kg (17 lbs.) total	not stated	"The carrier may not exceed 48cm in length, 32cm in width and 25cm in height."	150€ (intercontinental)
THAI	No (checked or cargo only)					
Turkish Airlines	Yes	1 carrier (note G)	6 kg total	not stated	45 cm x 35 cm x 23 cm	calculated as excess baggage
United	Yes (varies, see note I)	not stated	not stated	not stated	not stated	not stated
asdfsdfasdfasU.S. Airways	Yes (Costa Rica only)	1	not stated	not stated	17Lx16Wx8H (hard-sided) or 17Lx16Wx10H (soft-sided)	$125
Virgin Atlantic	No (checked or cargo only)					

NOTES

A. "A transport cage may contain up to five animals of the same species as long as the combined weight (including food and the carrier itself) does not exceed 10 kg." (Alitalia)

B. "If two animals are traveling in the same carrier, they must be the same species (two cats or two dogs, not one of each) and the pet and container can weigh no more than 20 lbs. combined." (American)

C. "Two pets of the same species and size may be allowed to travel in one kennel, provide they are small enough to fit into one kennel and are compatible. They will be charged as one pet." (Delta)

D. "In the case of animals of reduced size or weight, several of the same species may be admitted in a single container." (Iberia)

E. "Each passenger is allowed to carry only one pet. However, pets under 6 months of age can be transported in a pair using a single cage (the pair must be of the same breed, i.e., 2 dogs, 2 cats, or 2 birds to a cage)." (Korean Air)

F. "Each passenger may only bring one pet container on board. However, the pet container may contain more than one animal if they are from the same species and familiar with each other and have space to move inside." (TAP Portugal)

G. "Two pets of the same kind (two dogs or two cats) may be housed in the same kennel as long as they are accustomed to one another and the total weight of the kennel does not exceed 6kg." (Turkish Airlines)

H. Not U.K., Ireland, South Africa, Australia, New Zealand, Iceland, Hong Kong, UAE, Dubai, Dakar, Barbados, Jamaica.

I. "Rules for international in-cabin pet acceptance vary widely.... [T]o book international in-cabin travel for a pet, contact United Reservations."

U.S. CHECKED/CARGO PET TRAVEL

Airline	Checked pets OK?	Minimum age?	Largest kennel?	Weight limit (pet + kennel)	Fee	Reservation needed?	Cargo shipping available?
AirTran	no						no
Alaska	yes	8 weeks	Series 500 ("only accepted on Alaska Airlines flights 001-2999")	150 lbs. (heavier pets must travel as cargo)	$100	yes	yes
Allegiant	no						no
American	yes	8 weeks	Series 500 (not on MD-80s or Boeing 737s)	not stated	$175 (in the Americas); $150 (to/from Brazil); elsewhere, ask Reservations	no	yes
Continental	same as United						yes
Delta	yes	not stated	Series 500 (Series 700 as cargo only)	not stated	$200 each way	yes	yes (Series 700 max)
Frontier	no						no
Hawaiian	yes	not stated	Series 400 (B-717 planes) or Series 500 (B-767 and A330 planes)	70 lbs. (heavier pets must travel as cargo)	$60 (within Hawaii), $225 (elsewhere)	yes	yes
JetBlue	no						no
Southwest	no						no
Spirit	no						no

Airline	Checked pets OK?	Minimum age?	Largest kennel?	Weight limit (pet + kennel)	Fee	Reservation needed?	Cargo shipping available?
Sun Country	yes	8 weeks	Series 700	100 lbs.	$199 per flight segment	yes	no
United	no	8 weeks	Series 700 (except Series 500 on Boeing 737, United Express aircraft and some narrowbody aircraft)	250 lbs.	varies by weight and destination	yes	yes
U.S. Air	no						no
Virgin America	no						

INTERNATIONAL CHECKED/CARGO PET TRAVEL

Airline	Checked pets OK?	Minimum age?	Largest kennel?	Weight limit (pet + kennel)	Fee (each way)	Reservation needed?	Cargo shipping available?
Aer Lingus	yes	10 weeks	not stated	not stated	From U.S., not stated (call Pet Express at 1-866-PET-MOVE); from Ireland, 160€	yes	yes
AeroMexico	yes	not stated	not stated	not stated	$90 from/to U.S. ($80 pre-paid)	not stated	yes
Air Canada	yes	8 weeks	Series 700 ["292 cm (115 in) in linear dimensions (length + width + height)"]	32 kg (70 lbs.)	$105 USD/CAD from/to U.S.; $270 international	yes	yes
Air France	yes	15 weeks (8 weeks in "metropolitan France")	not stated	75 kg (165 lbs.)	200 from/to USA (EUR, USD or CAD, depending on country of departure)	yes	yes
Air New Zealand	yes (domestic flights only)	3 months	Checked pets: B737: 86cm H x 114cm W A320: 65cm H x 85cm W Link: 70cm H x 50cm W	no apparent upper limit	Checked pets: $75 NZ (up to 25 kg); $100 NZ (26 kg and over)	yes	yes (only option for international travel)
Alitalia	yes	3 months	not stated	75 kg	$260 from USA, 200€ to USA	not stated	not stated

Airline	Checked pets OK?	Minimum age?	Largest kennel?	Weight limit (pet + kennel)	Fee (each way)	Reservation needed?	Cargo shipping available?
American Airlines	yes	8 weeks	Series 500 (Series 400 on MD-80 (S80), Boeing 737, and American Eagle aircraft)	not stated	$175 ($150 from/to Brazil)	no	yes
ANA All Nippon Airways	yes	not stated	not stated	not stated	30,000 Yen ($300) from/to U.S.	yes	no
Asiana Airlines	no	8 weeks	Series 700? ("the three sides of the carrier may not exceed 246cm totally in length and its height may not exceed 84cm")	32 kg	not stated	not stated	no
British Airways	no						yes
Cathay Pacific Airlines	yes	not stated	unclear [extra fee charged if "larger than 158cm (62in)"]	32 kg (70 lbs.)	Charged "by piece system" from/to North America	not stated	unclear
Continental	same as United						
Delta	yes (cargo only for travel to or from South Africa, Hong Kong, or the United Kingdom)	not stated	Series 500 (Series 700 and larger crates okay in cargo)	not stated	$200 USD/CAD/EUR	yes	yes

Airline	Checked pets OK?	Minimum age?	Largest kennel?	Weight limit (pet + kennel)	Fee (each way)	Reservation needed?	Cargo shipping available?
Emirates	yes (except flights arriving in Dubai; also flight must be under 17 hrs.)	not stated	not stated	not stated	"normal excess baggage rates"	not stated	yes
Etihad	no						yes
EVA Air	yes	not stated	not stated	No restriction "with the exception of structural limitations on some aircraft"	"charged as excess baggage"	yes	no
Iberia	yes (except on IB5XXX flights)	not stated	not stated	not stated	"the rate applicable for excess baggage"	not stated	no
Icelandair	yes	not stated	Series 400? ("Maximum kennel dimensions are 92x56x71 cm")	32 kg	"the excess baggage charge applicable to the destination"	yes	yes
JAL	yes	8 weeks	not stated	not stated	"assessed according to the route"	yes	yes

Airline	Checked pets OK?	Minimum age?	Largest kennel?	Weight limit (pet + kennel)	Fee (each way)	Reservation needed?	Cargo shipping available?
KLM	yes	6 kg (13 lbs.) total	Series 700 (Series 500 on some aircraft)	75 kg (165 lbs.)	Varies by destination; there will be an extra charge if your layover at Amsterdam Schiphol Airport lasts 2 hours or longer	yes	yes
Korean Air (under "At the Airport," then "Baggage")	yes	8 weeks	Series 500? ["The total dimension (length + width + height) of the kennel should not exceed 246cm. (84cm or 33inch high on some aircrafts)"]	32 kg	"fixed excess baggage charges": KRW200,000/ USD200/CAD200 from/ to North America	yes	no
LAN	yes	8 weeks	not stated	not stated	"an excess baggage charge"	yes	yes
Lufthansa	yes	not stated	Series 500	32 kg	Varies by crate size and destination: $300 USD/CAD, 400 EUR for Series 500 from/to U.S.	yes	yes
Open Skies	yes	not stated	not stated	not stated	$195 or 125€	yes	no

Airline	Checked pets OK?	Minimum age?	Largest kennel?	Weight limit (pet + kennel)	Fee (each way)	Reservation needed?	Cargo shipping available?
Qantas	yes (domestic flights only)	not stated	Checked: Series 100 Cargo: Series 700 ("Must not exceed 84cm in height")	Checked: 20kg	Series 100=2 "pet packs"; applied against your normal baggage allowance	yes	yes (only option for international travel, inc. domestic sector of international flights)
Qatar Airways	yes	not stated	not stated	not stated	not stated	yes	yes
Ryanair	No						no
SAS	yes	not stated	Series 700+ ["If the cage size exceeds 158 cm (length + width + height), the price will double"]	not stated	€150/$200 intercontinental	yes	yes
Singapore Airlines	yes	6 months	not stated	not stated	"Pets - together with their containers - will be treated as excess baggage and charged accordingly"	yes	yes

Airline	Checked pets OK?	Minimum age?	Largest kennel?	Weight limit (pet + kennel)	Fee (each way)	Reservation needed?	Cargo shipping available?
Swiss	yes	not stated	not stated	not stated	400 USD/CAD, 300 EUR from/to U.S, for carrier larger than Series 100 (plus a Customs fee of CHF 88)	yes	yes
TAP Portugal	yes	not stated	not stated	45 kg (32 kg if travelling to/from/via USA, Hungary, France, Luxembourg, Netherlands)	€200 intercontinental (€30c if pet weighs up to 45 kg)	yes	yes
THAI	yes	not stated	Series 500 ("54 inches length, 27 inches height, 33 inches wide")	32 kg	calculated as excess baggage	yes	yes
Turkish Airlines	yes	not stated	not stated	not stated	unclear ("the piece concept applies")	yes	no
United	no						yes
U.S. Airways	no						no
Virgin Atlantic	yes	not stated	not stated	not stated	"depends on the size of its travel box"	yes	yes

B

Recommended reading

This is by no means a comprehensive list of the many available books and magazines that address pet travel. Instead, it's a list of the resources I actually use, with some notes about why I find them valuable.

PET TRAVEL GUIDES

➤ *A Guide to Backpacking With Your Dog* (Charlene LaBelle, Alpine Publications, Inc., 2004) and *Hiking With Your Dog* (Gary Hoffman, Mountain 'N' Air Books, 2002). There's some overlap between these two books, but they each have different strengths and are both good to have.

➤ *City Walks with Dogs* (Chronicle Books). Currently available jnt.im/236 for New York and San Francisco only; slightly out-of-date, but still a good purchase.

➤ *The Dog Lover's Companion to [Destination]* (Avalon Travel jnt.im/235). Series of guidebooks focusing on U.S. states or regions (*e.g.,* The Dog Lover's Companion to California jnt.im/237); some entries are dated, but I own them all.

➤ Doggy on Deck: Life at Sea with a Salty Dog jnt.im/234 (Penchant Press International, 2007). The sub-subtitle says it all: "Absolutely Everything You Need to Know Before Cruising with Fido."

➤ *Alastair Sawday's Special Places to Stay: Dog-friendly Breaks in Britain* (Alastair Sawday Publishing Co., Ltd., 2011). Guidebook of dog-friendly lodgings across England, Wales and Scotland selected for charm and quirkiness (everything from hotels and B&Bs to refurbished railway coaches and yurts), with references to nearby dog-friendly activities and pubs. Available through U.K. Amazon jnt.im/232.

➤ *Woodall's Camping and RVing with Dogs* jnt.im/233 (Woodall's Publication Co., 2009). A thorough, useful guide to camping and traveling with a pet in an RV or caravan.

PET-FRIENDLY VACATION IDEAS

➤ *Fido Friendly* magazine jnt.im/230. Extensive Travel section in each issue (while most of the articles focus on U.S. and Canadian destinations, other countries are also represented).

➤ *Sunset* magazine jnt.im/231. Not pet-focused, but the hotel and other vacation lodging ideas are well-chosen (focus on the Western U.S.); do your own research to see which are dog-friendly.

FIRST AID GUIDES

➤ American Veterinary Medical Association (AVMA) basic first aid procedures jnt.im/228

➤ "Doggy First Aid Tips jnt.im/229" (*Travels With My Pet*, 10/20/09). A sensible list of instructions from guest blogger Carol about handling basic pet ailments as well as emergencies.

➤ Randy Acker's Field Guide to Dog First Aid: Emergency Care for the Outdoor Dog jnt.im/227 (Belgrade, MT: Wilderness Adventures Press, Inc., 2009)

SCRAPS

➤ *Travels with Charley: In Search of America* (John Steinbeck). Travel literature classic describing Steinbeck's 1960 road trip across America with Charley, his Standard Poodle.